T011960-4

IRDS OF VOYAGEURS NATIONAL PARK

BIRDS OF VOYAGEURS NATIONAL PARK

A GUIDE TO THE

MINNESOTA-ONTARIO

BORDER COUNTRY

VOYAGEURS REGION NATIONAL PARK ASSOCIATION

Distributed by the University of Minnesota Press

Copyright 2001 by Voyageurs Region National Park Association

Published by Voyageurs Region National Park Association
514 North Third Street, Suite 104
Minneapolis, MN 55401

ISBN 0-8166-3899-3

The photography in this book belongs to Cornell Lab of Ornithology,
Bill Marchel, and Warren Nelson, unless otherwise indicated. The
drawings were donated by Matt Schmidt and John Pastor See page125
for complete acknowledgment.

Distributed by the University of Minnesota Press
111 Third Avenue South, Suite 290
Minneapolis, MN 55401-2520
http://www.upress.umn.edu

A Cataloging-in-Publication record for this book is available from the
Library of Congress.

Design by ThinkDesign Group
Printed in Canada by Friesens

This book is dedicated to Wallace (Wally) and Mary Lee Dayton, who have ardently and steadfastly supported Voyageurs National Park from its creation to the present day. We are grateful and indebted to them for all of their generous help. Some of the beautiful photographs in this book were taken by Wally and demonstrate not only his great talent as a photographer, but also his love of the birds of the northern border lakes country.

THE VOYAGEURS REGION NATIONAL PARK ASSOCIATION

Wally Dayton, 1970, camping on Lake Kabetogama at the time when Congress was considering the authorization of Voyageurs National Park.

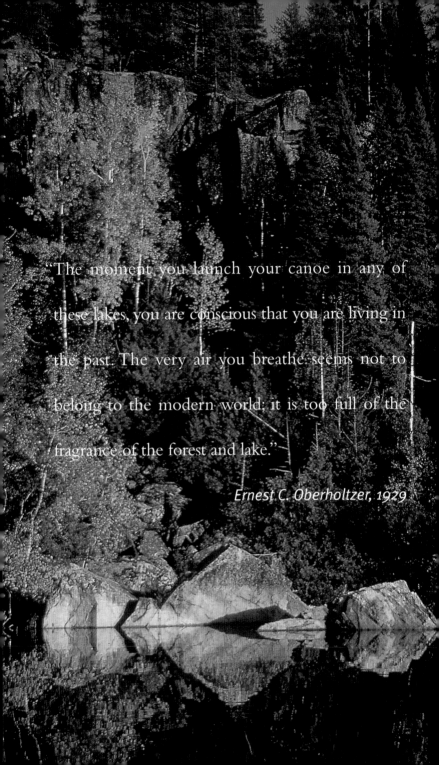

"The moment you launch your canoe in any of these lakes, you are conscious that you are living in the past. The very air you breathe seems not to belong to the modern world; it is too full of the fragrance of the forest and lake."

Ernest C. Oberholtzer, 1929

Voyageurs Region National Park Association Members

VRNPA Executive Committee and Board Members who lent their support during the creation of this book:

Nancy Albrecht	Joe Kotnik
Lee Barthel	Ann Ladd
Judy Bellairs	Doug Logeland
Richard Brown	Jim Martineau
Tom Clarke	Donald Nightingale
Linda Cloyd	Laura Oberst
Paul Cloyd	Beth Oschwald
Robert Corrick	John Pastor
F. Dallas Fogg	David Prince
Douglas Franchot	John Roth
John Grant	Larry Schwanke
Amy Hennen	Irene Serr
John Holmquist	Max Shemesh
Paul Johnson	Bill Underwood
Martin Kellogg	

Special Contributors:

Elmer L. Andersen	F. Dallas Fogg
Athwin Foundation	Parker Hall
Ford and Elinor Bell	Martin and Esther Kellogg
David and Vicki Cox	Doug and Mary Logeland
Bruce Dayton	Alida Messinger
Duncan Dayton	Kate Nielson
Edward Dayton	Quetico-Superior Foundation
Judson Dayton	Richfield Bank and Trust
Wallace and Mary Lee Dayton	Larry and Mary Schwanke
Olivia Dodge	Bruce Steiner
Douglas Franchot	Ellen Sturgis
Eco Trust	Evelyn Sweasy
Paul Egeland	William Sweasy, Jr.

A special thanks to John Roth, Susan Hilber, John Holmquist, Lee Grim, the National Park Service staff at Voyageurs, John Mathison, Paul, Linda and Lori Cloyd, Gordon Gelo, Wallace Neal, Gerald Rising, Jan Green, Jerry Neimi, Color Unlimited, Judy Kadash and LaFavor Pictures.

CONTENTS

Special Thanks   vii

Note to Readers by Barbara West   xi

Foreword by Leland H. Grim   xiii

Introduction   xv

The Habitats of Birds by John Pastor   1

Map of Voyageurs National Park   10-11

Illustrated Bird Anatomy   13

Voyageurs National Park Birds   15

Complete Checklist of Voyageurs National Park Birds   115

Bibliography   119

Index   121

About the Contributors   125

Ek Lake section of
Cruiser Lake Trail

DEAR READER

FOR ME, PERHAPS THE SINGLE most evocative aspect of Voyageurs National Park is its varied and rich bird life. Each season has its own different rhythms and sounds, and the sounds that are the most telling are the songs of the birds—some resident and some who just visit for a time in the spring or the fall. I am so pleased that the Voyageurs Region National Park Association has prepared this beautiful book to help all of us build our connections with the park through its bird life.

In the spring, local legend has it that there will be no more than three more snows after the gulls return. I know that after months of dark and cold, seeing the gulls gives me a special lift and sense that we really have made it through another winter. The spring also brings goldeneyes and their fabulous mating rituals and mergansers to nest in the just opened waters. White-throated sparrows with their distinctive call tell us that spring is melding into summer. And the loons are more than just Minnesota's state bird—their calls absolutely define a summer visit to the park. I don't like most things that interrupt my sleep—but loons hold a special place: there simply isn't anything like hearing loon calls across the still waters of the park's lakes no matter what time it is.

Hiking in the park early in the spring means warblers. I am still learning what to listen for and what to look for—but how many people have the opportunity to see and identify eight different species in less than half a mile, as I did on the Echo Bay Trail? I find the times that I identify a new bird are indelibly etched into my memory—I will always remember kayak trips that included my first Tennessee warbler and a particularly aggressive merlin. And I can still see that Cape May warbler in my mind's eye as he sat on a branch out over the waters of Cranberry Bay.

I think I may have the greatest affinity with the birds that stay here the year-round. Winter skis and snowshoes mean black capped chickadees and woodpeckers—downy, hairy, and pilated. But most of all winter means ravens—in pairs and in gangs—vocalizing and flying, demonstrating their wit and intelligence through blizzards and crystalline winter days alike. Sometimes, when it is very, very cold, it seems as if the ravens are the only friends to share the woods with.

It is a continuing joy to share the seasons in Voyageurs with birds—who come to the park because we protect a variety of habitat types and the ecological processes that sustain them. The world is changing—sometimes more quickly and permanently than we would like—and it is comforting to know that in fifty or one hundred years, Voyageurs will continue to be home or a stopping place to the birds in this book.

Sincerely,

Barbara West
Superintendent
Voyageurs National Park

For Voyageurs National Park information call Voyageurs National Park at 218-283-5821 or go to: www.nps.gov/voya/

Common
Mergansers

FOREWORD
Leland H. Grim

THIS HANDSOME GUIDEBOOK highlights 100 species of birds that can be discovered and enjoyed in Voyageurs National Park (Voyageurs). It was created by the joint efforts of ornithologists, biologists, volunteers, members of Voyageurs Regional National Park Association and VNP staff. It is not a complete field guide, but rather a pictorial guide. It includes general descriptions of the birds, indications of their relative abundance and seasonal distribution, a listing of the types of habitats they live in, and, most importantly tips about where they can most likely be discovered in and immediately around Voyageurs.

The book's contributors hope this attractive guide encourages visitors to go to the park's forested trails, lakes and ponds, and visitor centers to be inspired by the feathered creatures that live here. It is also their wish that visitors will want to know more about the birds and will ultimately seek out additional information about the park and its birds.

Voyageurs' biologists have been studying a complement of park bird species since 1973. There is annual information about the reproduction and distribution of bald eagles, osprey, great blue herons, terns, gulls, cormorants, loons, and red-necked grebes at park headquarters and visitor centers. Records and information about area birds have been kept by biologists from Rainy River Community College at International Falls, Minnesota, since 1967. Bird studies from the 1970s at Superior National Forest, some lands of which are now parklands, contributed to our knowledge of the southeastern portion of Voyageurs. Those sources of information were invaluable for determining the status and distribution of park birds.

Voyageurs began an ongoing monitoring system for determining the status and distribution of forest breeding birds in the mid-1990s. Point count routes have been established in a variety of forest types. The park will continue to increase the number of those routes and improve understanding of the ecological relationships between birds and their park environs. Voyageurs is also working with graduate students from a variety of colleges and universities to learn more about park birds.

Voyageurs just completed a four-year project to describe, classify, and map the vegetation of the park. The vegetation map in this book is a generalized product of that study and is the first broad use the park has made of the map. It will guide birders to specific vegetative types with their specific associations of bird species. That feature of the guide makes it a real plus for planning park birding trips.

Voyageurs offers a unique land and water interface, which gives visitors the opportunity to bird from watercraft and on foot. This makes it easy for visitors to interact with the great biodiversity of this water-based park. That richness is especially present in the new-world warblers that breed here.

Park staff would like to hear from you about your birding experiences while visiting Voyageurs. Please share them with us so we can help other visitors be awed and inspired about birds on the land and waters of the loons, eagles, and warblers. It is the park's mission to protect and preserve the bird resources for the enjoyment of the present and future generations of the nation. Enjoy your birding experience with our best wishes!

INTRODUCTION

WITH THIS GUIDE, WE INVITE YOU in to Voyageurs National Park and the Minnesota-Ontario border country. Its physical splendor will be your first welcome sign. This northwoods lake country is part of the Canadian Shield: a setting of lakes, peatlands, Boreal forests, and some of the world's oldest exposed rock; all of it courtesy of the last glacial age.

The border country has stories to tell. The life of the voyageur and the history of the Anishinabe and tales told by its life-long residents are only the beginning—tales grounded in the richness of the area's resources. Over time, various people came for the variety of the resources; from fish and wild rice, to beaver pelts, to timber, to the eco-tourism of today. That richness of the natural resources attracts a variety of wildlife and vegetation. This book is your guide to one of the many: an abundance of birds.

Why such abundance? It is a commitment to preserve unimpaired the natural elements which make up Voyageurs National Park, that provides a sanctuary for over 240 bird species. Some of them stay but two or three weeks—on their way to a further destination. Others make it their home for the summer or the winter season, and a few will rely on the border country resource to reside year-round. But whatever the length of their stay, because it is here, the birds will come and we can visit and watch in surprise and fascination. One hundred of these birds are found in this book, along with tips on where best to view them in the park.

National parks are created to preserve natural areas; areas that are but lightly touched by mankind, allowing the varied forms of wildlife to behave naturally in their native habitat. By the mid-1900s, Minnesota's border lake region from Lake Superior through the Boundary Waters Canoe Area was protected, leaving a portion of the "Voyageur's Highway" to the west. This portion, while recovering from an earlier generation's logging and dam building, was open to unrestrained private development and public misuse. The Voyageurs Region National Park Association was formed by private citizens in 1965 to foster the concept of a water-based national park as the best way to preserve this picturesque and unique resource. Today, the association seeks to protect the natural resources and habitats within the park through non-invasive activities. This book is part of that quest.

The individuals and institutions responsible for the existence of the border region as we find it today, are too numerous to thank. Rather than trying to do so here, we encourage you to visit the area. Refresh your spirit in what they have given us to enjoy, and leave it as you found it for your children's children to discover anew.

Join us! Call 612-333-5424 or go to: www.voyageurs.org

BIRDS OF VOYAGEURS NATIONAL PARK

THE HABITATS OF BIRDS
by John Pastor

ASKED WHERE THE GREATEST DIVERSITY of bird life is, most people would say the tropical forests, and they would be correct. Tiny Costa Rica for example—less than a fourth the size of Minnesota—has over 50 species of hummingbirds alone. Traveling northward, the diversity of bird life thins, until we reach the band of forest on the boundary of the northern hardwoods and boreal conifers stretching from Maine to the Upper Great Lakes area. This band has the greatest number of breeding bird species anywhere north of Mexico, on average 50 per twenty-five-mile survey route according to the International Breeding Bird Survey, sponsored by the USFWS and Canadian Wildlife Service. And in this band, Voyageurs National Park has some of the greatest bird diversity in North America with over 100 species known to breed within the park and over 100 more, non-breeding visitors.

The high diversity of birds at Voyageurs is a direct consequence of the high diversity of habitat, from the deep, open water of the large lakes to the shore side marshes and inland wetlands of the beaver ponds, to the great variety of upland forest of many ages. In addition, the forests of Voyageurs, although predominantly boreal conifers and deciduous species, are also at the northwestern-most end of the range of several oaks and other tree species of the more central hardwood forests.

Let's take a "birdwalk" across the Kabetogama Peninsula and discover something about the relationship of birds to their habitats. We shall start out by boat, canoe, or kayak in the middle of Kabetogama Lake. The deep waters here are the realm of the birds who fish. These include the common, red-breasted, and hooded mergansers; common goldeneyes; and of course the symbol of northern wilderness, the common loon. Breeding cormorants and non-breeding pelicans also make these waters their home, especially around small rocky islands where, along with ring-billed and herring gulls they will all congregate in flocks of 30 or more. Larger islands, especially those with large white pine for perches, are home to nesting bald eagles and ospreys who soar over the water looking for the unlucky schools of fish they spot near the surface. The osprey is the better fisher, but it is often robbed of its catch of fish by the bald eagle. And keep an eye out for a common tern, one of the most graceful of fliers, and the migrant Caspian tern, a larger relative.

As we move closer to shore, we leave behind the realm of the fishers and enter the shallow waters that are home to the dabbling ducks: mallards, green- and blue-winged teal, ring-necked ducks, pintails, and the rarer black ducks; these are often seen with the pied-billed, red-necked grebes. If we're lucky, we perhaps see a wigeon or the infrequently seen Western grebe, too. If diving ducks are the fishers of the waterfowl world, then these dabbling ducks are the vegetarians, with an occasional insect or crayfish for variety. The dabblers' diets of seeds and aquatic plants, especially wild rice, makes their flesh some of the most delicious of all wild game, and is the reason these ducks are prized by hunters while mergansers and other fish eaters are not.

The best place to see large rafts of dabblers, along with Canada geese, is in the prime habitat of Black Bay. It lies just west of the park boundary, with its shallow waters (less than six feet deep) and abundant wild rice beds to fatten on before the long, autumn migration to the Gulf Coast. Inside the park, Tom Cod and Cranberry Bays are excellent, too, and they share characteristics with Black Bay.

On the mostly schistose, gneissic, and granitic bedrock of the Canadian Shield, Voyageurs has few sandy beaches and mudflats, so it is deficient in the sandpipers and their relatives. Nevertheless, where there are beaches and mudflats we might see these small birds probing the mud and sand for worms or other morsels, leaving their footprints scattered about. Many of the sandpipers migrate through Voyageurs to their breeding grounds in the Arctic, but we see the spotted sandpiper throughout the summer, as it is one of the few sandpiper species that breeds in Voyageurs.

We are near shore now, so let's nose into one of the small bays created by the outlets of streams that drain the peninsula. Here is where we might catch a glimpse of one of the largest birds of Voyageurs, the great blue heron, wading in the quiet shallows and darting its bill into the water for small minnows, crayfish, or aquatic insects. Beaching our boat, we walk upstream for a short distance when we come upon a large beaver dam, holding back six feet or more of water, in the first of many beaver ponds. Peeking over the dam, we're likely to see the same dabbler ducks we saw near the lake shore. But the premier duck of the beaver pond is the wood duck, the male of which is one of the most spectacularly plumed waterfowl. The wood duck is likely to be nesting in a hole in a large, dead tree still standing in the pond after being

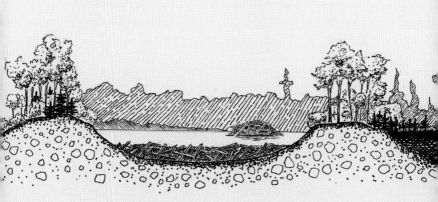

drowned when the dam raised the water. The hole itself will be rectangular, having been made by a pileated woodpecker. This, the largest of our resident woodpeckers, sports a spectacular red crest. Pause a moment more and you may hear a scream and rattling cry of the approaching kingfisher, flying past to perch on a branch sticking out above the water.

When the beaver fell and eat the available aspen around its shore they abandon the pond, while leaving the balsam fir, spruce, and pine behind. Without daily maintenance, the water flowing through and over the dam soon erodes it, especially if a river otter burrows into the dam to make a den. Eventually, the dam breaks and the wall of water rushes downstream, leaving behind a muddy meadow and a shrunken pond. Within a few years, sedge, iris, Canada bluejoint grass, and cattail spring from the mud to provide habitat for LeConte's and swamp sparrows as well as sedge and marsh wrens. These dense, grassy meadows also shelter the Virginia and sora rails and the American bittern, although these are more likely to be heard than seen. Near the edge of the meadow, willows, alders, and hazel provide song perches for white-throated and song sparrows and perhaps an occasional clay-colored or Lincoln's sparrow. A merlin, the swiftest of all birds of prey, except for the peregrine falcon, may have appropriated an abandoned crow's nest in the spruces left behind by the beaver. The Merlin will fly into the meadow with the deliberateness of a freight train and the adroitness of a downhill skier, catching smaller sparrows as well as dragonflies on the wing. Overhead, we may see a soaring broad-winged or red-tailed hawk, especially on those crisp, blue-sky days when they catch thermals rising from the ridge tops.

There is another type of wetland found in abundance in Koochiching

County and the western edge of Voyageurs, especially in the valley drained by the Rat Root River into Black Bay, and by the smaller streams draining into Tom Cod Bay. These are the large peatlands, which cover 15 percent of the land area of boreal regions. They are occupied by bogs of black spruce, sphagnum moss, leatherleaf, bog rosemary, rose pogonia orchids, pitcher plants, and many other strange and wondrous plants. The bird life of peatlands has not been well studied, perhaps because they are so inaccessible. Here we find a few species not likely to be found elsewhere, including the Connecticut warbler, which makes its nest from the sphagnum mosses, the palm warbler, and the great grey owl. It is possible there may be a flock of sandhill cranes here, migrating through and pausing for rest in the wetter areas (known as fens) which support sedges of a different species than in the beaver meadows.

We now climb into the uplands, and what a dynamic variety we have, beginning with hazel brush and the aspen-birch and jack pine forests that spring up after disturbances such as fires or logging, and under which spruce and fir are growing in the shade, eventually to replace the aspen and birch. These conifers, along with white or red pine that have survived fire and the lumberman's axe, form the old-growth forests of the park. This variety of coniferous and deciduous forest is constantly metamorphosing into another as fire and windstorms sweep through and recede. And the bird community inhabiting them is equally dynamic. The premier group claiming these forests as their own are the warblers, some 21 species of which breed in Voyageurs. That's half the warblers of eastern North America.

The chestnut-sided warbler rules the brushy scrub springing up after a fire

or along forest edges, and is easily recognized not only by rust colored streaks on its sides, but also by its call: "Pleased, pleased, pleased ta meet'cha!" This is reminiscent of the yellow warbler's "weet weet weet weet tsee tsee," but the yellow warbler is more likely to be found in wetter brush instead of the upland brush of the chestnut-sided. As the forest matures into saplings, the beautiful red-and-black American redstart may be seen; the redstart can also be seen on the edges of the forest opening where the fire disturbance ended or in the aspen saplings that sometimes spring up instead of fir after beaver fell the larger trees. As the forest matures and a complex canopy develops, various warblers begin to divide it up, concentrating their search for insects such as spruce budworm in certain portions to avoid competition with their relatives. These include, in progression from the forest floor upward, the yellow-rumped, bay-breasted, black-throated green, Blackburnian, and Cape May warblers, demonstrating that bird habitat is arrayed vertically as well as horizontally across the landscape.

As the aspen grow larger, heart rot enters and hollows their center, allowing access to insects sought by the pileated woodpecker. This opens up an entry hole, offering shelter to the boreal owl, a mysterious bird of the boreal forest. Outside of Voyageurs, foresters rarely allow aspen to reach this advanced age, preferring to cut them earlier for delivery to the pulp mills. For many years boreal owls were not thought to be resident in northern Minnesota, but nest sites are now known and Voyageurs may harbor a small breeding population. Rarely seen because of its nocturnal habits, the boreal owl is best discovered by its characteristic call which sounds like a soft, high-pitched bell or dripping water, heard best in the cold of a March or April night when it begins its mating season.

The upland forest is also home to a variety of woodpeckers. Besides the pileated, they include the familiar downy and hairy woodpeckers and the flicker and yellow-bellied sapsucker which can be seen in almost all forests, to the more elusive black-backed or three-toed woodpecker that specializes on the bark beetles that attack mature spruces and firs. Experienced birders can distinguish the different drumming sounds these woodpeckers make, from the loud rapping of the large pileated—like someone hitting a tree with a hammer—to the subdued pecking of the smaller species. These forests also provide a home to the ovenbird; the red-eyed and solitary vireos; flycatchers sallying forth from the tops of trees to catch flying insects, a sharp-shinned hawk chasing a Cooper's hawk, the nuthatches and the brown creeper climbing up tree trunks, the ruby-crowned and golden-crowned kinglets, the boreal and black-capped chickadees, the gray jay, a blue jay flying with an acorn in its bill, the crossbills scattering the seeds of spruce and pine, and, always, more warblers.

As you can see, Voyageurs is rich in bird life and offers many lessons in the relationships between birds and their habitats. In our imaginary walk today, we met more than 60 species. A pair of binoculars, a field guide, a little knowledge of habitats, along with abundant curiosity, sandwiches and coffee in a knapsack, that's all you need for an enjoyable day of birding, year-round.

VOYAGEURS NATIONAL PARK BIRDS

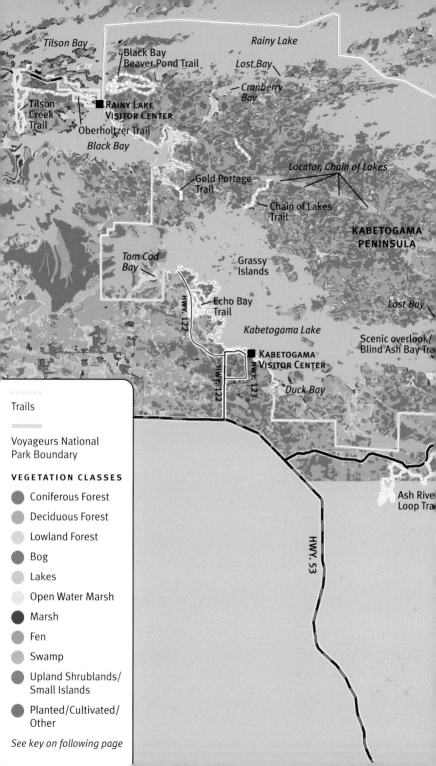

Tilson Bay

Rainy Lake

Black Bay
Beaver Pond Trail

Lost Bay

Tilson
Creek
Trail

Cranberry
Bay

■ RAINY LAKE
VISITOR CENTER

Oberholtzer Trail

Black Bay

Locator, Chain of Lakes

Gold Portage
Trail

Chain of Lakes
Trail

KABETOGAMA
PENINSULA

Tom Cod
Bay

Grassy
Islands

Lost Bay

HWY. 122

Echo Bay
Trail

Kabetogama Lake

Scenic overlook/
Blind Ash Bay Tra

HWY. 122

HWY. 123

■ KABETOGAMA
VISITOR CENTER

Duck Bay

Ash Rive
Loop Tra

HWY. 53

Trails

Voyageurs National
Park Boundary

VEGETATION CLASSES

- Coniferous Forest
- Deciduous Forest
- Lowland Forest
- Bog
- Lakes
- Open Water Marsh
- Marsh
- Fen
- Swamp
- Upland Shrublands/
  Small Islands
- Planted/Cultivated/
  Other

See key on following page

5   0   N   5   **10 Miles**

Voyageurs National Park

MINNESOTA

ONTARIO
MINNESOTA

CANADA
UNITED STATES

Anderson Bay

Mica Bay Trail

Cruiser Lake

Mica Bay

KETTLE FALLS VISITOR CENTER

Cruiser Trail

Namakan Lake

H RIVER SITOR CENTER

Sullivan Bay

Sand Point Lake

Little Trout Trail

Grassy Bay

VOYAGEURS NATIONAL PARK

Crane Lake

Vermilion Gorge Trail

CRANE LAKE VISITOR CENTER

ORR VISITOR CENTER
Bog Walk Trail
(not shown, ₁₁₁ city of Orr)

KEY TO MAP

(in reference to the Voyageurs National Park map, pages 28 and 29)

For purposes of simplicity, we have grouped the park's vegetation types into ten communities to help you find the birds listed in this book. As you will note, some of these birds will be found in a particular community while others can be found in many communities.

WETLANDS

BOG: Characterized by continuous carpet of sphagnum moss, soil is wet and nutrient poor. Ringed by Tamarack and Black Spruce.

SWAMP: Northern White Cedar, Black Spruce, and Tamarack growing on spongey sphagnum moss carpet, alder grows at shrub level.

FEN: Wet spongy peatland covered mostly by grasslike sedges, which typically grow in tussocks.

MARSHES: A shallow basin of half a foot to three feet of standing water. Typically covered by herbaceous aquatic plants, such as cattails, bulrushes, and waterlilies.

OPEN WATER MARSHES: Similar to Marshes but with breaks in water covering aquatic plants, wetter than a marsh and water tends to be deeper.

OPEN WATER: Lakes, beaver ponds, and streams.

UPLANDS

LOWLAND FORESTS: Areas dominated by poorly drained soils that include ash, cedars, and aspen.

UPLAND SHRUBLANDS: Less than 25 percent tree cover.

DECIDUOUS: Forest or woodlands largely dominated by deciduous trees.

CONIFEROUS: Forest or woodlands largely dominated by conifers.

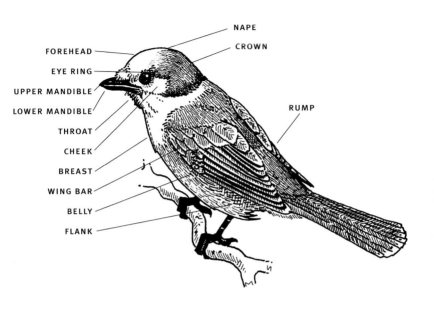

NAPE

CROWN

FOREHEAD

EYE RING

UPPER MANDIBLE

LOWER MANDIBLE

THROAT

CHEEK

BREAST

WING BAR

BELLY

FLANK

RUMP

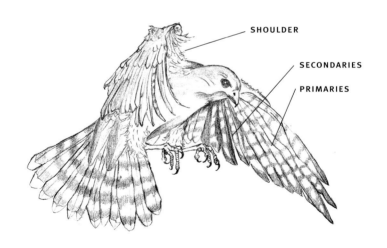

SHOULDER

SECONDARIES

PRIMARIES

KEY TO BIRD SIDEBARS

SIZE
This will tell you the general size of each bird.

HABITAT DESCRIPTIONS *(see Map Key on page 12)*
Bog
Swamp
Fen
Marshes
Open Water Marshes
Open Water
Lowland Forests
Upland Shrublands
Deciduous
Coniferous

OCCURRENCE
This will tell you how much of the year each bird can be found in the park: permanent resident, Summer resident, Winter resident, migrant or transient.

The second part refers to each bird's abundance, for residents or visitors and not for migration: Common—Seen daily, Uncommon—Seen at least weekly, or Rare—Found a few times each season.

IDENTIFICATION
This will give you some distinguishing traits to help you quickly identify each bird, based on their coloring, personality and/or song.

COMMON LOON
Gavia immer

In *The Singing Wilderness*, Sigurd Olson wrote, "I knew as I stood there waiting that once a man had known that wild and eerie calling and lost himself in its beauty, should he ever hear a hint of it again, no matter where he happened to be, he would have a vision of the distance and freedom of the north."

Loons are handsome black and white duck-like birds that periodically dive under the water to fish. Although they resemble ducks they are actually in their own family, Gaviidae. Loons can be seen swimming and diving in most of the four main lakes and inland lakes of the park. With their large bodies (28-36 inches), black and white backs and sharp bills, they are hard to confuse with any other bird.

Loons are a migratory species in the park, nesting in early June and leaving by October. They often hide their nests in the vegetated shorelines of small lakes and back bays of undeveloped lakes. Research in Voyageurs National Park found unnatural fluctuations in seasonal water levels contribute to low loon reproduction rates in the larger lakes. Inland lakes (with natural water level fluctuations) support relatively normal loon reproduction rates in the park. During the summer, the young chicks can be seen swimming close to their parents or catching a ride on their parents' backs.

TIP: Listen at night to the call of the loon, often described as yodeling, quavering laughter and falsetto wails. Watch them in quiet back bays of the park from a distance. Caution: Nesting loons are very sensitive to disturbances such as watercraft.

SIZE: 12 – 15 inches

HABITAT: Marshes and open water marshes

OCCURRENCE: Summer, Uncommon

IDENTIFICATION: Smaller than a duck, dives

PIED-BILLED GREBE
Podilymbus podiceps

These small diving birds are fairly solitary, and may hide in marshes by slowly sinking until only the head is above water. Pied-bills are twelve to thirteen inches long, with a small stocky brown body and short stout bill. The bill is white, adorned with a striking black ring around it.

Pied-bills aptly dive underwater, feeding on fish, mollusks, and aquatic insects, propelling themselves with their feet. An early migrant, they may appear in Voyageurs before the ice is melted. Their courtship display involves calling back and forth and sometimes in unison.

Like other grebes, their young can swim shortly after hatching and ride on their parents' backs, even when they dive. The young are quite conspicuous, and don deep brown and white stripes, appearing to look like recently escaped convicts. Both parents feed their young and they may have two broods in a year. They nest near marshy ponds and outlets.

TIPS: When the ice first goes out, look for Pied-billed grebes around the many islands and quieter shorelines of the park. By mid-June they will have more private grassy quarters, such as Duck Bay, Grassy Bay, Black Bay, and Cranberry Bay.

SIZE: 12 – 15 inches

HABITAT: Open water

OCCURRENCE: Transient, uncommon

IDENTIFICATION: Bright "ear plumes", dives

HORNED GREBE
Podiceps auritus

This migrant water bird primarily eats fish, tadpoles, and insects. Like other grebes, they are talented "hide-and-go-seek" players, by using their innate talent of hunkering down while swimming, exposing only their heads. Horned grebes tend to be solitary feeders, diving and propelling themselves with their feet underwater. In the summer, both sexes have reddish-brown necks and sides with golden ear tufts and black heads. They are around 13 inches long, and are slightly bigger than Eared grebes. In winter, they have dark gray backs and heads with white necks.

It is a treat to see their elaborate courtship displays involving both male and female. They may be seen scurrying side by side carrying weeds, or sitting very erect, using a variety of calls and whistles. When paired, they will build a nest of wet plant material in shallows or marshes. Young grebes swim soon after hatching and are often seen sporting a ride on their parents' backs.

TIP: Look for horned grebes as soon as the ice leaves the major park lakes. When they first arrive, they can be found in open bays and swimming along the parks many islands and rock outcroppings. As summer approaches, look for them back in the grassier bays of the parks, namely Tom Cod, Black Bay, Cranberry Bay, Duck Bay, and Grassy Bay.

SIZE: 18–20 inches

HABITAT: Open water marshes and open water

OCCURENCE: Summer, uncommon

IDENTIFICATION: Long rufous neck, dives

RED-NECKED GREBE
Podiceps grisegena

This is the largest of the grebes commonly seen in Voyageurs and one of the oldest bird species in terms of evolutionary relationships. Red-necked grebes earn their name from their breeding-plumage: their lower neck and upper parts black with upper bill black and lower bill yellow, and their eyes red. This bird is an excellent diver and swimmer. It has the unique ability to submerge its body (studies say air is expelled from their bodies and dense feathers) leaving only its neck and head, giving the appearance of a colorful periscope. Their necks are long and graceful.

They make their nests on floating vegetation debris, anchored in grassy bay areas in water deep enough for them to dive into if threatened. Like other ducks, grebes will molt in July and August, losing their bright plumage, thus concealing themselves during a time when they are unable to fly. Grebes typically are seen in flight only during migration, preferring to dive and swim when threatened.

TIP: In the spring, after ice out, red-necked grebes are easy to find and watch swimming and diving around the multitude of islands in the park's four major lakes. If you visit during the summer, look for them in the grassy areas of Black Bay, Duck Bay, Cranberry Bay, and Grassy Bay. This is their preferred habitat.

SIZE: 55 – 70 inches
HABITAT: Open water
OCCURRENCE: Transient, uncommon
IDENTIFICATION: Very large white bird, long bill, flies in formation

AMERICAN WHITE PELICAN
Pelicanus erythrorhynchos

This large water bird is white with black primaries and a bill many times longer than its head. The American white pelican averages 62 inches long with a 108 inches wing span. According to Robert Jansen's *Birds in Minnesota*, the American white pelican is rare in the park area and tends to be non-breeding while in the area. A fibrous plate in the upper mandible, which is shed after their eggs are laid, notes breeding American white pelicans. The crown and nape become grayish during the chick feeding period. Breeding stage birds are often seen in Voyageurs.

An American white pelican has several distinguishing characteristics. From a distance it appears white with a long orange bill. In flight, you can spot black on its primary wings, see its long neck tucked back against its upper back with its bill jutting straight out and its orange webbed feet hanging back under its large body, resembling a large cargo plane in flight. These are not diving birds; rather they circle schools of fish and, using their bills with fibrous pouches, scoop them up and slowly swallow what they have collected in their pouches.

TIP: Look for them as soon as the ice is out of the big lakes. They often fly in V-formation. American white pelicans gather on rocky outcroppings early in the morning on Rainy Lake and on rocks on the northern side of Lake Kabetogama during the day. They will share their rocky islands with gulls and cormorants. They leave the park by September for their fall migration.

DOUBLE-CRESTED CORMORANT
Phalacrocorax auritus

The double-crested cormorant is a large black diving waterbird, about 33 inches long with a 54 inches wing span. It has a small orange pouch, four-toed webbed feet and a long neck. The double-crested cormorant's bill is about the length of its head with a hook on the end. They are known for their diving skills and will use their wings to increase their ability to catch fish. They are considered to be a nuisance to fishermen because of their capacity to catch fish. In 1928, Minnesota Department of Natural Resources Commissioner Carlos Avery placed them in a hunting season. Over 1200 double-crested cormorants were reported to have been killed that year.

Unique characteristics of the double-crested cormorant include the way they look in the water and the places you can find them in Voyageurs. When floating on the water their large body is quite submerged making the long neck and head seem like a periscope. During mating season, the double-crested cormorant will grow two light-colored curly tufts or crests on the back of its head. They build their nests on rocky islands, called rookeries, in Voyageurs, using sticks, and will share their rocky islands with gulls.

TIP: The double-crested cormorant can be found on rocky islands and rock outcroppings throughout Voyageurs' large lakes. Look for rookeries on Rainy Lake, halfway between the park entrance on Rainy and the Brule Narrows and on rocks in front of the Kabetogama Visitor Center. They can be found perched on top of buoys in the park and will be seen sharing space with pelicans.

SIZE: 39–52 inches

HABITAT: Marshes, open marshes, and open water

OCCURRENCE: Summer, common

IDENTIFICATION: Long legged wader, flies with neck folded

GREAT BLUE HERON
Ardea herodias

These large graceful birds have often been called "cranes" from earlier popular depictions in ancient Oriental paintings. Herons, however, have slightly longer bills and fly with their heads hunched back near their shoulders. They have long, sleek necks and large bills. They are very patient hunters, and are often seen standing still or walking slowly in the shallows. They are formidable, standing 50 inches tall with grayish-blue bodies with white heads and a black stripe above their eyes. Great blues eat small fish, frogs, birds and snakes by rapidly striking them with their bill. Their diet is highly variable, for they have been seen stalking small mammals as well.

They will breed in colonies on large platform-like nests made of sticks and lined with grasses and plants. Males decide on the site, and try to attract females there. The nests are built mostly by the females in trees or shrubs, and can be as high as 70 feet off the ground. Both parents feed their young by regurgitation.

As if posing for the perfect picture, they are often found hunting at the edge of a pond or marshy area. Moving very slowly, they wait for a fish to swim near and then strike it with a rapid jab of its bill. This bird is highly adaptable, and can be found throughout North America. They are not friends with park gulls who will pester and chase herons out of an area.

TIP: Look for solitary herons in Black Bay, Tom Cod Bay, Duck Bay, Grassy Bay and Cranberry Bay.

SIZE: 25 – 32 inches

HABITAT: Open water, deciduous, and coniferous forests

OCCURRENCE: Summer, common

IDENTIFICATION: Glides in circles, wings slightly arched into a "V"

TURKEY VULTURE
Cathartes aura

Flying in the sky, from a distance, turkey vultures portend to be of similar size to the bald eagle (69 inch wing span). But look closely: the turkey vultures wings are held upward in a slight V, its flight feathers are silver-gray, its linings are black and the red head is featherless. Unlike the eagle, the turkey vulture's talons are too weak to catch prey. Instead, they feed on carrion and garbage. Rather than regular flapping of its wings, look for them to rock back and forth in flight. They do not build nests but lay eggs in an enclosed area like a cave or a hollow log. Unlike most birds, turkey vultures have a well-developed sense of smell, allowing them to find carrion by odor. These birds are regulars in Voyageurs National Park. Just remember V for vulture when you see a large bird in flight. Look for them to return to the park in April. Many vultures can be found soaring together.

This family of birds is known from fossils dating back millions of years. These vultures, referred to as New World vultures, are not related to hawks and eagles but from a group yet to be identified. While touted for this beautiful soaring, much has been noted of this ungainly appearance when perched, their hissing calls, their ability to smell yet eat carrion and their "disgusting habits of ejecting at the intruder, the putrid, foul smelling contents of their stomachs" (Roberts, Volume 1, page 296).

TIP: Look for turkey vultures soaring over the park's treetops, perched on tall snags, or at the water's edge.

SIZE: 22 – 45 inches
HABITAT: Open water
OCCURRENCE: Transient, uncommon
IDENTIFICATION: Long black neck with white throat

CANADA GOOSE
Branta canadensis

Canada geese have black heads, neck and feet, a brownish body with a lighter chest, and range from 35 to 45 inches in size. The black head is offset with a white chinstrap and the tail has a white U-shaped mark. They are commonly known for their flying in V formation and for their loud, melodious honking. This honking is actually a duet of male and female calls. Since there is no difference in plumage between sexes, one must rely on behavior and calls, the males making an "ahonk ahonk" and the females making a "hink" call.

They can be upland feeders, grazing on grass and other green herbage as well as acorns, berries, corn and grain. In shallow water, they will search the lake bottom for a variety of aquatic creatures, as well as tubers, root stalks and other water plants.

While they are abundant in Minnesota in general, they are less so in Voyageurs, residing there only in the summer months. They build their nests on the ground near open water or on small hummocks. They go through one molt a year at midsummer, becoming more elusive until they can fly again when they will form flocks in preparation for their fall migration. Canada geese remain together for as long as they both live. When one dies, the other will find a new mate within a year. It is the only member of its family ever to nest in Minnesota.

TIP: Listen for them as they fly overhead and look for them in the grass bay areas like Black Bay, Cranberry Bay, Grassy Bay, and Duck Bay.

SIZE: 18–27 inches

HABITAT: Marshes and open water marshes

OCCURRENCE: Summer, common

IDENTIFICATION: Green headed dabbling duck, drab female

MALLARD
Anas platyrhynchos

The male mallard duck has a green head, white neck ring, a chestnut breast and a gray body while the female is a mottled brown with a white tail. Both have purplish-blue inner wing feathers. They are known as wary, fast, flying birds.

They are dabbling, omnivorous ducks that eat pond weeds and grasses, tree seeds and grains, as well as aquatic insects and small fish, frogs, and mollusks. This is one of the most abundant ducks in the world. The Mississippi flyway has been referred to as the mallard flyway due to the number of mallards to be found.

The quacking sound associated with mallards is a call made only by the female. The male whistles during courtship and at other times makes a nasal "rhaeb" sound. Mallard plumage includes one incomplete molt in late summer to early fall. The midsummer molt transforms the male plumage to that of the female, which happens as the male leaves the incubating female. The full fall molt transforms the male into its best-known coloring, just in time to start its active fall courtship. By winter, mallards have decided on a mate as compared to other species that wait until late winter to start the courting process.

TIP: Look for mallards in Black Bay, Duck Bay, Grassy Bay, and dabbling around the many park islands and shorelines. Mallards prefer water less than 16 inches deep with aquatic plants, ideal for this dabbler.

SIZE: 14 – 18 inches

HABITAT: Open water marshes and open water

OCCURRENCE: Summer, common

IDENTIFICATION: White striped bill, black male drab female

RING-NECKED DUCK
Aythya collaris

This diving duck is a strong, fast flier. It can be seen feeding in woodland ponds, and when disturbed, seems to take flight by rising directly up. The name of this stunning bird is very misleading, for the ring around their neck is very difficult to detect. Coined the "ring-billed" duck by hunters, this name seems more suitable, as there is a prominent ring around the tip of both the male and female's bill. Ring-necked ducks have peaked heads, and the male's white crescent sides show vividly against their otherwise gray-colored bodies. Females are mostly brown, with a white eye ring and a faint white line extending back from their eye. In flight, a noticeable gray stripe can be seen on their primaries.

These ducks dive a few feet deep, and eat a variety of aquatic plants and insects. Courtship begins in early winter, when the male displays by swimming forward with their heads rapidly nodding. After pairs have been established, they build a nest on a dry clump of brush or a floating mat of vegetation, close to open water. It looks like a shallow bowl of grasses and weeds, lined with down. Unlike most ducks, a unique behavior of the female is that she stays with their young until they are able to fly.

TIP: Look for these ducks in Black Bay, Cranberry Bay, Duck Bay, and Grassy Bay.

SIZE: 15 – 20 inches

HABITAT: Open water

OCCURRENCE: Transient, common

IDENTIFICATION: Blue bill, mottled wings, rounded head, noisy in flight

GREATER SCAUP
Aythya marila

Common to the boreal forest lakes and bogs, Voyageurs National Park is part of the greater scaup's spring and fall pass–through areas. The blue bills, white sides and what appears to be a light gray back, which is actually black and white barring, distinguish the male scaup.

It is very difficult to distinguish between greater and lesser scaup. Their heads from a distance or in poor light appear to be black, but like a male mallard seen in sunlight, their heads will be a glossy green (for greaters) and glossy purple (for lessers). Their breasts and tails are black. Both female types are generally brown with a darker brown head and a white patch at the base of the bill. There are slight differences in size, bill shape and length of white secondaries that can be seen in flight. Add to these small differences, the chance of interbreeding (found to happen in the duck community) and these distinguishing marks are even tougher.

Differences between scaup: the greater scaup are on average ten percent larger than lesser scaup. Greaters have a more rounded head, a bill that is quarter inch longer and have white secondaries that extend toward the wingtip that can be seen in flight as compared to the lessers who have white secondaries as seen in flight with gray primaries.

TIP: In the early spring, right after ice-out in late April, look for hardy scaup in open bay areas, bobbing and diving for food. By mid-Spring, greater scaup move north. Greater scaup will return to flock with lessers in the late fall on the large park lakes.

SIZE: 15–18 inches

HABITAT: Open water marshes and marshes

OCCURRENCE: Transient, common

IDENTIFICATION: Blue bill, mottled wings, angular head

LESSER SCAUP
Aythya affinis

The lesser scaup, nicknamed "little blue bill," can be found, spring through fall in the boggy lake areas of the boreal forest. They are said to enjoy feeding on the exotic zebra mussel. This scaup seems to be the more popular of the two found in the park as compared to the greater scaup, although attempts to distinguish between the two types are hard enough that this information may be skewed. The male lesser scaup has the same markings as the greater scaup—white side panels, blue bill, gray back, dark head and tail. The lesser scaup's forehead is slightly taller, making the head look oblong with a peak towards the rear of the crown. Its bill is .25 inches shorter than the greater. From a distance, if you determine the scaup markings, a best guess would be a lesser scaup, according to reports from the park area. Particularly in the fall as the ice gets ready to form, large flocks of lesser scaup will land in the middle of the park's large lakes, staying until the lakes ice over.

Courtship takes place in the spring and is begun with bill bobbing, nipping at each other, and diving, swimming, and emerging together.

TIP: Visit the park's lakes and in particular Black Bay in late October and early November to view large flocks of lesser scaup before they depart for warmer waters. These are the last waterfowl to migrate through the park in the fall. Lesser scaups have also been spotted in the spring on the large beaver pond on the Chain of Lakes Trail.

AMERICAN GOLDENEYE
Bucephala clangula

The common goldeneye is a large diving duck that has been known to call Minnesota its home year-round. The female has a white breast with gray-white wings and upper body with a dark bill. The male has a dark head with round white spots on each side of its face, a black band running down its back, and a white breast. Listen as they fly overhead: their flapping wings make a whistling sound. Their choice of food includes water-related bugs, insects, dragonfly nymphs, and small fish. They are successful breeders in Voyageurs, having eight to fifteen chicks in one hatching. The downy chicks will try to dive and swim away from you on approach only to bob right back up to the water's top.

TIP: Look for American goldeneye in shallow grassy bays and near shorelines of Voyageurs. Black Bay on Rainy Lake, the Grassy Islands in Lake Kabetogama, and Grassy Bay in Sand Point Lake are good spots. There is a good chance they will be swimming in front of your tent or cabin site.

SIZE: 16 – 19 inches

HABITAT: Open water

OCCURRENCE: Summer, common

IDENTIFICATION: Disproportionately large white crest with black border, drab female

HOODED MERGANSER
Lophodytes cucullatus

The long, thin, toothed bills of this merganser are used to catch fish when diving, earning its name the "little fish duck," because it is smaller than the common merganser. The male is conspicuously handsome with a black full crested head with a white center, white breast with a black ribbon running through the lower part and a pale brown belly. The female is brownish over-all with a full brown crest. They are beautiful divers, lifting their front off the water then arching their back and diving, in their search for fish, mollusks and water insects with a small portion of plant matter. The hooded merganser prefers woodland ponds and backwaters, making the shallow, back bays of Voyageurs an ideal summer setting. Thomas Roberts noted "Their flesh is hardly edible and they are of little economic value but not necessarily harm-ful." Most fish-eating birds consume, chiefly, small fish that devour the eggs and fry of more valuable species, making the hooded merganser a benefit to humans.

TIP: Quietly boat into Duck Bay, Grassy Bay, or Cranberry Bay in late spring and sum-mer and you will see these mergansers. At ice-out time in the spring, they can be seen paddling and diving around the many park islands.

SIZE: 22–27 inches
HABITAT: Open water marshes and open water
OCCURRENCE: Summer, common
IDENTIFICATION: Long white bird with black head, gray female with orange head

COMMON MERGANSER
Mergus merganser

Common mergansers are large mallard–sized diving birds, about 25 inches long. Their long red bills slope gently from their forehead. They deftly catch fish, insects, and crustaceans with their narrow hooked bill and saw-like bill. Male common mergansers have a white body, white flanks, black backs, and shiny green heads. Females, on the other hand, have slightly crested bright chestnut colored heads with grayish bodies. They are the largest of all mergansers with graceful necks and show pointed wings when they fly.

Common mergansers nest between boulders, roots of trees, or in tree cavities. Their nests are lined with down and weeds. The wooded lakes of the border country offer wonderful nesting and feeding areas for this skilled diving bird.

TIP: In spring, after ice-out, look for these birds floating on the large lakes or saunter-ing along island shorelines with their mates. In the summer, they can be spotted in inlets and creeks and other quiet spots throughout Voyageurs with their chicks.

OSPREY
Pandion haliaetus

The osprey is a large raptor, 21 to 24 inches in length, often called the "fish hawk" due to its habit of diving feet first into the water for fish, its only food. Ospreys in Voyageurs nest in the very tops of dead trees, usually in beaver ponds off of inland drainage and lakes. They are a migratory species, spending the breeding season in the park and the winter in Central and South America. The park is home to some 20 to 30 pairs.

Look for a large bird hovering over shallow bays and then suddenly plunging into the water. Once a fish is caught, the bird will laboriously flap its way out of the water, carrying the fish in its talons to the nest or a nearby perch. Ospreys have a broad black cheek patch and a dark patch on the underside of their wings.

TIP: Some typical fishing spots for ospreys in the park include Echo Bay or Sullivan Bay on Lake Kabetogama, Cranberry Bay or Lost Bay on Rainy, or Grassy Bay on Namakan. When soaring, ospreys can be distinguished from eagles because their wings do not stretch out flat, but are angled.

SIZE: 30–31 inches

HABITAT: Open water, deciduous and coniferous forests

OCCURRENCE: Summer, common

IDENTIFICATION: large brown bird with white head, immature mottled

BALD EAGLE
Haliaeetus leucocephalus

Voyageurs National Park is a great setting to watch this majestic bird as an aerial performer, as an architect of large nests, for its sheer size, and even its role of thief, opportunist, and scavenger. One of the many benefits of having VNP is the chance to study these birds in a natural, undisturbed setting. Eagle research in the 1990s found an average of 30 active nests, seagulls and fish as primary food source and the presence of PCBs (heavy metal chemicals, byproducts of high powered generators) in their body fat. Studies show eagles in Voyageurs produce at (.0 to 1.42 fledglings per nest) compared to neighboring Chippewa National Forest (1.4–1.9 fledglings per nest).

With a good pair of binoculars, eagle nests can be found by scanning the tops of white pine trees. Look for nests, on average six feet in diameter and four to eight feet deep with branches as large as two inches in diameter.

NOTE: During their nesting season, it is imperative that you keep a distance of over 250 feet from the nest. This bird does not tolerate human presence.

Eagles mate for life and take joint responsibility for incubating, brooding and feeding their young. The female is larger than the male, which is the best way to distinguish sex. Typically two eggs are laid.

TIP: Look for tall white pines on the water's edge where eagles will nest and roost. They can be seen soaring above the tree lines. Look for them being chased by or chasing ospreys.

SIZE: 13–15 inches

HABITAT: Deciduous and coniferous forests

OCCURRENCE: Summer, common

IDENTIFICATION: Mottled brown and white mid-sized hawk

BROAD-WINGED HAWK
Buteo platypterus

The broad-winged hawk is a perching hunter of the deep woods. Given that they are woodland birds, you often hear broad-winged hawks before you see them. Listen for their slightly descending whistle: "sigee."

This bird of prey has good hearing and keen, "hawk-eyed" vision which is used for finding their prey. They eat small mammals, amphibians, reptiles, birds, mice and voles. They hunt by waiting for prey from a perch then quickly diving to catch it with their talons. The shape of a broad-winged hawk is made for this type of hunting. This is characteristic of the buteo hawk family, which has broad wings and a short tail meant for soaring and looking for food.

They construct nests on a small platform of sticks lined with bark and moss or they will use the nest of another hawk, crow, or squirrel, in the lower part of a conifer or deciduous tree. They usually lay two to three eggs. The nest is often near a clearing and in the same area as their previous year's nest. Nesting hawks are quiet and hard to find.

To recognize them, look for the broad black and white bands on the adult tails as compared to the red-shouldered hawk that has narrow white bands. Broad-winged hawks are about the size of a raven, the female being larger than the male, and they are day travelers, dependent on thermals as they form.

TIP: Listen for these hawks as you walk the park's trails or down adjacent roads or sit beside one of the many beaver ponds with a good pair of binoculars and wait.

SIZE: 9 – 12 inches

HABITAT: Deciduous and coniferous forests

OCCURRENCE: Summer, common

IDENTIFICATION: Petite colorful falcon, hovers

AMERICAN KESTREL
Falco sparverius

Kestrels are the smallest falcon, and are often seen perched on roadside wires or hovering over fields. They are very skilled hunters, and wait patiently to pounce on an unsuspecting grasshopper, mouse, bird or reptile. Formerly, they were called "sparrow hawks" because of their size, about 10 inches tall, and for sparrows as their chosen prey. They have blue-gray wings and head, rusty back, black tail band, and distinctive black mustache.

Kestrels generally use tree holes originally excavated by other birds for nesting. These sites are found in February, when the male starts feeding the female. Most vocalizations occur near the nest site, and consist of a loud rapid "klee-klee-klee-klee." Females are responsible for nest preparation and incubating. Because of the divided responsibilities, it is common to see solitary kestrels. After incubation, both parents are involved with feeding their young.

TIP: Take a trip to a beaver pond in Voyageurs and sit quietly at the forest edge. Kestrels can be seen flying over the ponds. They are also found along the roadside on your way into the park, perched on wires and in trees along resort roads, looking for their next meal.

SIZE: 10–14 inches

HABITAT: Open water, deciduous and coniferous forests

OCCURRENCE: Summer, uncommon

IDENTIFICATION: Small brown and tan falcon

MERLIN
Falco columbarius

The merlin gets its nickname, the "bullet-hawk" from its fast acceleration and speed. Merlins, like the falcon family in general, are medium-sized raptors with long, tapered, pointed wings, shaped like isosceles triangles maiking them intimidating hunters and flyers. When roosting, a merlin's wings are noticeably shorter than its tail. Large eyes and keen eyesight are distinguishing traits of falcons. They locate their prey by sight and catch them with their feet. Merlins nest in the same site for several years.

These falcons are slightly larger than pigeons, ten to fourteen inches long with a large head. Their bodies have a fuller chest and are heavier than their slower-flying relative, the kestrel. They are known as a wilderness bird of the boreal forests and the tundra. Look for them in the afternoon, when they do most of their hunting. They look for prey, including grackles, sparrows, and finches, from a perch, most often found on the edge of a conifer forest clearing.

Listen for its high pitched call of "klee klee klee." They are highly aggressive during breeding and migrating seasons. Females are dark brown above and heavily streaked in their under-parts. Males are metallic blue above with lighter, finer streaks below. Males are smaller than the females. These birds, another victim of DDT, are reportedly increasing in numbers.

TIP: They can be seen sitting on roadside wires and perched on snags along roads leading to park resorts. If you want an up-close look at a merlin, visit the Wildlife Museum, Highway 53 in International Falls.

SPRUCE GROUSE
Falcipennis canadensis

These chicken-like birds are found singly or in groups on coniferous forest floors, quietly pecking as they look for pine needles and buds for food. They fly but only for short distances and are very approachable, thus earning the name "fool's hen."

Like the ruffed grouse, the spruce grouse has cycles of high and low populations. They are permanent residents of northeastern Minnesota. These ground dwelling birds have strong short bills. Males have a dark throat and breast dappled with white and a red fleshy comb. Females are browner with barred under-parts. Both have dark tails with chestnut tips.

Courting males show off by erecting their combs and fanning their tails. The female makes clucking sounds and the male beats his wings, either in the air or more effectively on a hollow log.

TIP: Look for spruce grouse when hiking the Mica Bay portage, particularly in the fall. When they are in a cycle of high population, you will see them on either side of the trail.

SIZE: 9–11 inches
HABITAT: Upland shrublands and deciduous forests
OCCURRENCE: Summer, common
IDENTIFICATION: running shorebird, broken wing display

KILLDEER
Charadrius vociferus

This common shorebird is aptly described as "vociferous." About the size of a robin, slightly bigger that a spotted sandpiper, the killdeer is easily recognizable by its ongoing loud call "kideah" sounding much like a non-enunciated "killdeer."

The two bands of black across a white breast, the white neck and forehead with brown on the upper body provide easy markings for identification—as long as you can find the birds in their shoreline habitat where these features blend in with their surroundings.

They are also known for their broken-wing act, which they use to distract intruders from their nest. They will also try to fool intruders by repeatedly running a distance on the shoreline, and settle themselves on some pebbles as though to cover their eggs and/or nest. This will continue until the unwanted guest gives up—probably having never neared the Killdeer's actual nest which is nothing more than a shallow area of scraped soil, holding 3-5 black-and brown-blotched eggs. Both adults help incubate and tend the nest. Killdeer are known to return in early spring to the park area, able to endure any unexpected bard spring weather. Killdeer are more sociable with each other than spotted sandpipers.

TIP: Look for these birds in the Gold Portage area or on the pebbly beaches of the hundreds of park islands.

SIZE: 7.5 inches

HABITAT: Open water

OCCURRENCE: Summer, common

IDENTIFICATION: brown spotted wader, twitches its tail

SPOTTED SANDPIPER
Actitis macularia

The little spotted sandpiper, also known as the teeter snipe is 7½ inches long and can be found in the shorelines of Voyageurs National Park. These birds are typically seen individually or in pairs but do not flock.

The spotted sandpiper gets its name from its round dark spots on its white underbelly during the breeding season. Otherwise, its belly remains white and its upper back is a pebble brown color. Traits of a spotted sandpiper include quick teetering movements as though it is constantly nervous. On the ground it makes a mellow "peet-weet" call and calls out a series of weet notes when in flight.

Its nest, like its plumage, is camouflaged on rocky or pebbly beaches, and can be made up of twig, grass, leaves, bark and pebbles. The brownish-black speckles and spots on a creamy-colored base camouflage the 1 to 4 eggs laid.

In flight, the spotted sandpiper will beat its wings in stiff, quick, rapid movements, uttering a subdued weet. It will swim and even dive when it feels it is necessary.

TIP: Look for this pretty little fidgety bird on sandy, pebbly park shores.

SIZE: 10.5 inches
HABITAT: Sedge fen and lowland forest
OCCURRENCE: Summer, common
IDENTIFICATION: Mottled brown and white with long straight bill

COMMON SNIPE
Gallinago gallinago

The snipe is a very solitary bird of wet fields and bogs, and is difficult to spot. They feed mostly on worms, but they also burrow for insect larvae, spiders, and leeches. Their flexible bills are adapted to detect and nab underground creatures.

This long-billed shorebird, stands about 11 inches tall, and can be seen flying in a zigzag pattern while giving a bizarre raspy harsh call. Its mottled brown body and striped head is distinctive in flight. This bird is a popular game bird and will flush only when predators are very close.

The female builds a well-hidden nest in a clump of grass, equipped with a canopy-like structure of grasses, leaves, moss, and sometimes overhanging plants. If threatened, she will crouch low and raise her spread-patterned tail to distract predators. Snipes are special sights to see especially if you catch a male flying high overhead in daytime with outer tail feathers vibrating in quivering hoots to attract a female.

TIP: Look long and carefully throughout high grasses along the Oberholtzer Trail for the snipe's head. In the spring, they could be there nesting and mating.

SIZE: 11 inches

HABITAT: Upland shrublands and deciduous forests

OCCURRENCE: Summer, common

IDENTIFICATION: Chunky long-billed ground bird

AMERICAN WOODCOCK
Scolopax minor

American woodcocks are very chunky, with short stout legs and long straight fairly flexible bills. They have large dark eyes and head, short neck, and a dark mottled colored back, which allows marvelous protection among dead leaf patterns on the ground. The bill is covered with a soft membrane and a sensitive tip adapted to probing worms in soft earth. Their eyes are widely spaced, allowing it to watch for danger even with its bill burrowing in the soft earth. They are shy and inhabit grassy marshes and moist woodland floors, where their nests are well hidden in forest thickets.

Males display at night and in the early morning. This "sky dance" is fantastic. They circle spirally up calling a "twitter-itter-itter" and then they elaborately swoop down to attract females. After these nuptial flights, a female will visit the area, copulate, and return to her nest to care for the eggs, and eventually raise the young on her own. Their call is normally a nasal "peent," that can be heard mostly in the spring.

A widely hunted game bird, woodcock numbers have greatly decreased.

TIP: Look for woodcocks on the Echo Bay Trail especially in the spring as the female is rearing her young.

SIZE: 18–20 inches

HABITAT: Open water

OCCURRENCE: Transient, uncommon

IDENTIFICATION: Black line through beak, yellow legs

RING-BILLED GULL
Larus delawarensis

These gulls are among the most common in the area and are very sociable. They nest in colonies, and are very gregarious. These are the birds you may have seen scavenging for scraps in restaurant parking lots or picnic areas. They are about 17 inches long, with a wing span of 48 inches. Their plumage differs only slightly from summer to winter. Their heads and bodies are white, wings gray with black primaries that are dotted with two white spots. They have yellowish-colored legs, and show their characteristic black ring near the tip of their yellow bill.

During courtship, males feed the females, and then proceed with a little dance, accompanied by the female. Stretching their necks, they will alternately face each other and suddenly turn away. The established pair will build a nest of grasses, twigs, and moss on the ground. If the clutch size exceeds four eggs, another female may "share" the nest. Both parents feed their young.

Their diets may vary. They can be seen in fields foraging for grubs and earthworms. However, because they are so opportunistic, they also eat insects, grain, rodents, and whatever they may find while combing garbage cans. They are also known for stealing food from other birds. These gulls are also part of the park eagle diet.

TIP: Listen for their mewing call, higher pitched than the herring gull and for their yellow legs and feet as they fly overhead or sit on the many rocky islands and outcroppings of the park's lakes.

SIZE: 23–26 inches

HABITAT: Open water

OCCURRENCE: Summer, common

IDENTIFICATION: Yellow bill with red spot, pink legs

HERRING GULL
Larus argentatus

One of the largest gulls, this 25-inch long gull has about a 58-inch wing span. Gull coloring is highly variable; however during breeding, these gulls have white bodies, and white patches on their otherwise gray wings whose tips seem to be dipped in black ink. Their legs and feet are pink, and their bill is yellow with a bright red spot.

In the spring, these gulls pair up. The older previously mated birds tend to arrive first and reestablish their spots in the nesting territory. Younger birds that are breeding for the first time conduct wonderful head bobbing and neck stretching courtship displays. After pairs have been established they will attempt to find a nesting area on the periphery of the already established nesting colony. Both adults contribute to the nest building and feeding of their young. The common call of this gull is a "klew, klew," and they build their nests on the ground from weeds and grasses.

TIP: The rocky outcroppings on Voyageurs lakes provide ample viewing spots for these gulls. Look at their pink leg coloring for the easiest indicator of this gull and listen for their lonely call, heard from far away.

SIZE: 13 – 16 inches

HABITAT: Open water

OCCURRENCE: Summer, uncommon

IDENTIFICATION: Black capped, forked tail

COMMON TERN
Sterna hirundo

This tern is the most abundant one on the continent. They are mostly gray, with white breasts, a black cap, and measure about 14 inches. They have bright red bills usually tipped black. Their pointy wings and forked tails distinguish them from gulls, as well as their feeding technique.

When feeding they sail across the water, hover, and plunge-dive into the water after their prey. Terns are often seen carrying a fish or tadpole back to their mate who is watching over the nest. Males and females both attend to the nest, but shortly before the little ones hatch, the female stays dutifully at the nest while the male "fetches" meals. After the chicks are born both adults feed them.

They nest on bare ground including the rocky lake islands in the park, in low grasses, cattails, and dead vegetation. They nest in colonies, and have decreased in population due to competition with gulls for nesting sites and predation by great horned owls. The gulls in Voyageurs are notorious for taking over tern nesting sites.

When predators are in sight, the colony often takes "to wing" calling loudly until the danger has passed. Normally, they have a rather loud "keee-r-r-r" call.

TIP: Currently there is a small tern colony near the Sheep Islands in Lake Kabetogama. In the spring of 2000, two black terns were also seen in this area.

SIZE: 20 inches

HABITAT: Deciduous and coniferous forests

OCCURRENCE: Permanent, common

IDENTIFICATION: "Who-cooks-for-you" song, black eyes

BARRED OWL
Strix varia

As dusk settles and you sit at the edge of the mature lowland forests in Voyageurs National Park, a barred owl is apt to be heard, giving a eight-hoot long: "Who cooks for you? Who cooks for you all?"

This 21-inch-long bulky-looking owl with dark eyes and barred upper breast is a common, year round resident in Voyageurs National Park. The Voyageur mature forests suit this owl with a cleared understory, hollowed trees for its nest and few great grey owls to threaten it.

The female is typically the larger of the sexes with a slightly higher pitch in her voice than the male. All other characteristics are similar. It is known to respond to recorded or human-voiced hoots. Finding their daytime roosts is difficult, as they leave no trace of food or fecal scattering at their nest sites. Two to three white eggs are laid each year, with the owls returning to their same nesting sites yearly. Due to cramped nest quarters, the young will often leave the nest before they can fly.

TIP: Take an early evening walk down the Kabetogama Lake Road, the Ash River Road, the Vermilion Gorge Trail or the Oberholtzer Trail. Listen for the barred owl to hoot its famous questions. It may respond to you if you ask the same questions in return.

SIZE: 10 inches

HABITAT: Upland shrublands, deciduous and coniferous forests

OCCURRENCE: Summer, common

IDENTIFICATION: In flight, pointed wings with white bars

COMMON NIGHTHAWK
Chordeiles minor

During the twilight hours, look for the common nighthawk with its erratic flight and angular wings as it feasts on swarms of flying insects. This bird, mottled in brown, gray and white, is a member of the whip-poor-will or "goat-sucker" family and not the hawk family. They are eight to ten inches long with a wingspan of two feet. Their call is a nasal "peent" or "beermp". During courtship, males make power dives, resulting in a loud "boom" as it ends its descent. The power dives tend to be done over the male's chosen nesting area.

Nighthawks have short bills that open into a very wide mouth. This gape makes up 15 percent of its total body area, making it very effective in scooping flying insects, including mosquitoes, beetles, June bugs, moths, and flies. Their large wings have patches of white out from the elbow. They have a large tail, dark body, and big eyes. The male has a white throat patch and the female's patch is buff. Males have a white tail band, and the female's tail is dark.

Their nest site is a scratched patch of ground. Approaching a female on her nest will result in her hissing with her mouth wide open and flaying her wings out. They have been found to eat over 500 mosquitoes or 2100 flying ants in a day. They arrive in and depart from the Park with these flying insects, traveling in early evening.

TIP: Look for nighthawks in rocky openings next to wooded areas during the peak summer months. If you are staying at a park resort, they can be seen near outdoor lights, feeding on the insects attracted to light.

SIZE: 3-5 inches

HABITAT: Upland shrublands, deciduous and coniferous forests

OCCURRENCE: Summer, common

IDENTIFICATION: slightly larger than a bumblebee, long bill

RUBY-THROATED HUMMINGBIRD
Archilochus colubris

This beautiful, busy, tiny bird is the only hummingbird found in these parts, or indeed east of the Great Plains. It is approximately 3½ inches long. The male, which is smaller, weighs about the same as two paper clips. Both males and females have metallic green backs and head crowns with whitish gray underparts. The male declares a spectacular brilliant red throat, black shin, and dusky green sides. When caught in the right light the brilliant red throat is awesome. The female has a white chin, buff sides, and a tail dipped in white.

Because of their size, hummingbirds are very active feeders, and you can sometimes hear but not see them. With wing beats of 80 times per second, you especially hear them whirring about during early spring when courtship abounds. Hummingbirds eat flower nectar, as well as insects and spiders. They tend to like red tubular blossoms, and hover over the flowers while feeding.

Males usually arrive at nesting sites before the females, and defend a territory of about a quarter of an acre. When the female arrives, the pair exhibits courtship displays of diving and shuttling back and forth after one another. Their calls consist of a loud chip-chip, or a twitter. The established couple will build two to three tiny nests about 10 to 20 feet high on a horizontal limb, constructed of plant down, bud scales, spider webs and lichen.

TIP: There is a good chance you can spot them feeding on Jewelweed blooming in wet areas off of the Echo Bay Trail.

SIZE: 13 inches

HABITAT: Open water marshes and open water

OCCURRENCE: Summer, common

IDENTIFICATION: Spiked crest, rattling call, dives from perch

BELTED KINGFISHER
Ceryle alcyon

The belted kingfisher is an easily spotted bird over the beaver ponds and brooks of Voyageurs. From a distance it looks like a compact Blue Jay with an oversized head, a ragged hairdo and a heron-like bill. Its slate blue head, white ringed throat, slate blue ringed breast, and slate blue and black wing feathers are hard to miss in flight. Add a red patched breast to the female and you have a very bright bird. Its sudden dive into the water in search of fish, which it will eat whole, shows the power behind its head and bill.

The belted kingfisher will also be noisy like a blue jay, uttering a loud dry rattle. If you are paddling along a stream in their feeding territory, they will fly ahead of you, calling as they go in an attempt to escort you out of their average 500-foot-long shoreline territory.

Belted kingfishers typically make their home in exposed sandy banks by digging tunnels and making nests back in dry cavities. They will perch on dead branches no more than 100 feet from their tunnel. They will also make their homes in tree cavities, but never too far from their water source.

TIP: Look for these birds in the springtime as they fish throughout the day for food for their young. They can be found on the Gold Portage flowage, and the beaver ponds on the Chain of Lakes and Cruiser Lake trails of the Kabetogama Peninsula.

YELLOW-BELLIED SAPSUCKER

Sphyrapicus varius

Yellow-bellied sapsuckers are pretty birds in appearance, with a red-crowned head, blackish back, white wing patch, and white rump. Their breasts are pale yellow and they have a black crest. The male has a red throat while the female's throat is white. They are a summertime visitor, arriving in Voyageurs' forests by late April and leaving in late August to early September. They will nest in the same tree but will excavate a new hole that barely fits them each new year. The male returns first, tappng the nesting tree to attract its mate. Their nesting tree, likely an aspen, is found near punctured trees, making food available through the summer for themselves and their young. They have a loud, irregular drum and sound like a blue jay in its loud cat-like calls.

Of all the woodpeckers found in the park, the yellow-bellied sapsucker can create the most threat to the health of the forest due to the number of holes punctured in a single tree, which cause bug infestation and decay. They puncture holes just deep enough into the trees to reach the sap layer. A sapsucker leaves its trademark by circling a tree with its holes. As the sap supply dwindles, they puncture a new set of these circles up the tree and out onto larger limbs. Insects will stick to the sap providing extra food for the sapsucker as they return to these seeping holes.

TIP: Look for a yellow-bellied sapsucker tree-pattern of circumscribing holes and search the immediate area for their nest. While inspecting sapsucker holes, look for hummingbirds enjoying the sap, too.

SIZE: 6 inches

HABITAT: Deciduous and coniferous forests

OCCURRENCE: Permanent, common

IDENTIFICATION: Small, relatively tame woodpecker

DOWNY WOODPECKER
Picoides pubescens

The little downy woodpecker is one of the smaller and less shy woodpeckers. Their black and white coloring is similar to the hairy woodpecker, and they are found in the same forest areas as the hairy. The downy forages for insects on smaller trees. A red head patch distinguishes the male. If you can study the black and white patterns on their heads, each downy can be individually identified. Like other woodpeckers in Voyageurs, the male and female downys lead separate lives from mid-summer to early fall yet they stay in the same territory varying in size from 5 to 25 acres. Only lack of food will force them to leave the area. Listen for their drumming in late winter, signifying territory and an effort to communicate with their mate. This drumming will continue into spring, gradually establishing the extent of the couple's range. The drumming is a duet—the male and female continually drum to each other.

Mates use separate drumming posts. For these woodpeckers it is crucial that the male and female agree on a choice of tree to excavate for a nest site. If agreement is not reached, breeding will be unsuccessful. Many nest sites will be started before a final site is chosen.

TIP: In the spring, walk through the Echo Bay trail, the Blind Ash Bay Trail or the Vermilion Gorge Trail and look for fresh chips beneath a tree. Downy excavation occurs in the morning. The three types of tapping to listen for are courtship drumming, continual regular loud excavation work, and quieter, irregular tapping for food.

SIZE: 9 inches
HABITAT: Deciduous and coniferous forests
OCCURRENCE: Permanent, common
IDENTIFICATION: Robin-sized black and white woodpecker, long beak

HAIRY WOODPECKER
Picoides villosus

The hairy woodpecker is a beautifully marked black and white bird, similar in color to the downy woodpecker, with differences in size and bill shape, back color, and call. The hairy has a longer chisel-shaped bill. The male has a red head patch. These woodpeckers are shyer than its relative, the downy, and larger, 9 inches, or robin size. They can be found in deciduous forests, feasting on insects, including harmful ones like wood-boring beetles, thus contributing to the health of the forest. Berries are also a part of their diet. Like other woodpeckers, they will hammer on head limbs during courtship and to mark their territory. They also have a call like a sharp "peek," which is louder and different from the downy's dull-sounding "pik" call. They can be found year-round in Voyageurs and will typically excavate a cavity in a deciduous tree, done by both sexes and lay up to four eggs in late spring. Like most woodpeckers found in VNP, hairy woodpeckers have strong feet (two toes forward, two back), skull and bill which absorb the shock of repeated pounding on hard wood, and a long, coiled tongue, compared in length only to its ant-eating cousin's tongue, the northern flicker. They are known for stiff tail feathers, which brace them as they pound trees in search of insects. In flight, look for a bouncing beat and flight pattern, common to all woodpeckers.

TIP: Listen for the hairy woodpecker in the spring as you hike park trails, including the Blind Ash Bay Trail.

SIZE: 9 inches

HABITAT: Coniferous forests

OCCURRENCE: Permanent, uncommon

IDENTIFICATION: Yellow cap, black back

BLACK-BACKED, THREE-TOED WOODPECKER
Picoides arcticus

Northern Minnesota is on the extreme southern tip of the black-backed, three-toed woodpecker's eastern range. It is largely associated with the northern tundra and Pacific Rockies. It's close relative, the three-toed woodpecker (*Picoides tridactylus*), though rare, may also wander into Voyageurs, so double-check. The black-backed appears more solid black than the three-toed, which has a mottled, white back. The black-backed is the size of a robin, soot-black in color. The males and immatures have a yellow crown near the front of their head and white undersides.

Both are somewhat tame, though shy and less conspicuous than the other woodpeckers in the park. Their habits are also similar: favoring burned-over, logged, and swampy environments. Even in their preferred habitat, these birds are not common or predictably encountered. Like the rest of their family, they use their high-powered chisels to destroy tree bark and gather grubs and beetles. Generally silent, their notes sound more like the whimpering of a small mammal than the call of a woodpecker.

TIP: Look for these woodpeckers in the late winter and early spring on the Blind Ash Bay trail, when snow is still on the ground. Large patches of bark stripped from conifers, easily spotted on the snow, is a good indication that these birds are active in the area. Look around the Crane Lake area and inspect conifers around your tent and/or cabin. Listen for them as they pull of the bark looking for their next meal.

SIZE: 12 inches

HABITAT: Upland shrublands, deciduous and coniferous forests

OCCURRENCE: Summer, common

IDENTIFICATION: Colorful woodpecker, in flight underside of wings bright yellow

COMMON OR NORTHERN FLICKER
Colaptes auratus

This large brown woodpecker enjoys living on the forest's edge, using dead or dying trees for its home and the adjoining field for its favorite food source: ants. This flicker has a softer and curved bill as compared to other woodpeckers, requiring it to search for softer trees to excavate for home. Its tongue is one of the longer woodpecker tongues, except the hairy, coated with a sticky substance that can easily catch many ants at a time. Flicker stomachs have been found to hold 500 to 5,000 ants.

During courtship, flickers are actively darting from ground to tree and back. They are also very noisy, using many different calls. These birds jointly excavate a nest hole, incubate, and feed their 6-8 young. Nests can be found 2-20 feet above ground or higher.

As this woodpecker flies, look for yellow under-wing feathers. Their white lower back is easy to spot in flight. The male has a black or a red mustache patch. Some of the more common calls include "flick-a, flick-a," "wicker wicker wicker" or "wick wick wick." Look for flickers returning to the park with robins and grackles.

TIP: Look for flickers along the Echo Bay Trail and the Oberholtzer Trail, flitting from low tree branches to the ground and back. In the spring, they sit on roadside wires with their white lower back to identify them as they fly off. Easily frightened off by grackles, juvenile flickers can be spotted poking through moss in search of insects.

SIZE: 17 inches

HABITAT: Deciduous and coniferous forests

OCCURRENCE: Permanent , common

IDENTIFICATION: Large woodpecker with red crest

PILEATED WOODPECKER
Drycopus pileatus

The pileated woodpecker, with a wingspan of 30 inches, is the largest woodpecker commonly seen in North America. Its large black-backed body with a red head, long powerful bill, and a flash of white under-wings make for a prehistoric image as it flies silently through dense forests. Its head, spine, and bill are strong enough to chip off tree bark pieces as large as a human hand, most likely in search of carpenter ants. Other interesting facts:

- Their brain is surrounded by an air pouch to protect it from the intense hammering of the head and bill;
- It can hear carpenter ants, their favorite food, under tree bark.
- They even can find these ants as they lie dormant in the winter.
- They use their long, sticky, fringed tongue to lap up beetle larvae.

Look for rectangular holes in trees, their trademark when they look for insects. They carve out a new nest hole every year. Other insect-loving birds with weaker bills seize the old holes. Their trademark sound is a repeated accelerated rolling tapping on a tree. Look for pileated woodpeckers in dense forests, areas where tree heart rot is occurring or where storms have downed old trees, thus introducing insects that start the decomposition process.

TIP: While walking the Echo Bay Trail on a warm March morning, we startled a pileated woodpecker in the woods. After flying off to a new perch, it called out, "wucker-wucker-wucker" protesting our presence.

53

SIZE: 6 inches

HABITAT: Deciduous and coniferous forests

OCCURRENCE: Summer, common

IDENTIFICATION: "Pewee" song, white wing bars

EASTERN WOOD-PEWEE
Contopus virens

A member of the flycatcher family, this medium sized flycatcher can be seen darting out from a perch to catch insects in mid-air and fly to a perch. Its head is large for its body size, a dark olive-gray color above, a dull white throat, darker-white-gray-olive breast, and dull-white to pale yellow underparts. Adults have a dark upper mandible and dull orange lower mandible. The bill is broad-based and flat, designed for catching insects. Their song is a slow plaintive, "per-a wee," often heard with a "pee-yer." Pewees sing at dawn and dusk, continuing into the evening after other songbirds stop. They are better known for their song "pee-a wee," than by their looks. They are typically heard before they are seen.

Eastern wood pewees live in woodlands, in the leafy middle story of mainly deciduous trees. Sometimes they will be found in a mixed deciduous coniferous area, but seldom in a coniferous woodland. Listen for pewees around meadows, beaver ponds, clearings and roadsides. They eat flies, wasps, bees, winged ants, and moths. Males sing in the spring to defend their territory. Their small nest, which looks like a bump on a branch, is 15 to 45 feet high in deciduous trees and is lined with lichens.

TIP: Listen for Pewees as you hike the Chain of Lakes or Cruiser Lake Trails, the Echo Bay Trail or the Ash River's Beaver Pond overlook or while on the Rainy Lake Visitor Center's beaver pond interpretive walk.

SIZE: 5.25 inches
HABITAT: Deciduous and coniferous forests
OCCURRENCE: Summer, common
IDENTIFICATION: White eye ring

LEAST FLYCATCHER
Empidonax minimus

Flycatchers are notorious for being difficult to tell apart. Least flycatchers are no exception, for their olive-gray coloring above, with white wing bars, white throats, light gray breasts and soft yellow bellies are similar to many other flycatchers. These flycatchers are about 5¼ inches long with proportionately large heads, and large eyes that bear bold white eye rings.

Like other flycatchers they are skillful fliers. They are often seen perched on branches, then flying out, dipping and soaring to catch aerial insects, only to return to their perch. They seem fond of forest edges, which provide them with open feeding areas as well as shelter among the nearby trees. You can spot them feeding in open woods and aspen groves, and find their nests in deciduous groves.

Their nest is a compact cup of grasses and bark strips, lined with animal hair, feathers, and plant down. Nests are usually built in the vertical fork of a tree. The male chooses the females during courtship. They are territorial and nest in loose colonies.

TIP: As you walk the park trails, look for these birds in the relatively open parts of forests and open woodlands where there is a well established shrub layer.

SIZE: 7 inches

HABITAT: Deciduous and coniferous forests

OCCURRENCE: Summer, common

IDENTIFICATION: Twitches its tail

EASTERN PHOEBE
Sayornis phoebe

These seemingly tame birds are easy to observe, and mark the coming of spring with their early arrival. They are about 7 inches tall, are brown above, whitish below, with a dark bill. They have no distinguishing wing bars, and may show a yellowish belly in late summer. Their head is the darkest part of their body.

Phoebes are often found perched on a branch ready to fly and catch insects in midair. They also pick insects off the ground, and eat berries during the cooler months. They are very skillful flyers and often return to the same perch between beak-filling forays. They also have a habit of wagging their tails and giving a soft "tee-bee" call.

Upon arriving at the nesting site males protect their territories by chase and song. After the female arrives the song may only be heard in the early morning. Females build the nest, usually along a stream, woodland edge, or often under a bridge. It is made of a solid base of mud, built up with leaves and grasses.

TIP: Listen early in the morning for phoebe's song when the ice goes out of the lakes. They are common and can be found along forest edges and heard as you walk park trails.

SIZE: 9 inches

HABITAT: Deciduous and coniferous forests

OCCURRENCE: Summer, common

IDENTIFICATION: Yellow belly, loud "peent"

GREAT-CRESTED FLYCATCHER
Myiarchus crinitus

Woodland bigmouths, great crested flycatchers can be heard in the tree-tops, shrieking their characteristic melodic "wheep!" Often it is one of the only birds heard while walking through the forest during hot summer after-noons. It bursts swiftly from branches and dashes out after insects, then returns to the same tree. When the males arrive each spring in North America, they establish relatively large territories and defend them aggres-sively against other males, often fighting in midair and ripping out oppo-nents' feathers. The great crested is easier to identify than many other flycatchers. It is colorful and large, and also the only eastern flycatcher, which nests in holes, whether natural tree cavities or woodpecker holes. They have even been known to nest in mailboxes.

It primarily feeds on flying insects: flies, bees, mosquitoes, wasps, beetles, and also berries. The female usually lays 5 or 6 eggs, which she will incubate for up to 15 days.

Look for a large flycatcher that is robin-sized; brownish on back and cap, gray throat, and yellow belly. Its crest is not obvious. Easier to hear than see, they often remain high in forest canopy.

TIP: You can hear these birds when hiking the Echo Bay Trail and the Vermilion Gorge Trail on an early spring morning.

EASTERN KINGBIRD
Tyrannus tyrannus

The eastern kingbird is typically noted for its fearless pursuit of larger birds in defense of its territory, yet allowing birds its size or smaller to nest within its territory. Often found sitting erect on an open branch or fence wire, these birds can be spotted by their white breast, blackish head, slate-gray back, and white-banded tail feathers. Kingbirds are known to chase crows, ravens, hawks, and vultures, picking at them as they drive them out of their territory. They are also known for the male's aerial tumbling performance after chasing off intruders. It has no real "song" per se but will scream as it pursues larger birds and in early morning or early evening they will utter a high-pitched "kitter kitter kitter." Like other birds in this family of flycatchers, the eastern kingbird exhibits the flycatcher traits of darting out from a perch, catching insects in flight, and darting back to a perch. Its bill is broad-based and flat so when opened, it is wide and ready to capture many insects at a time.

Look for the female to build the nest, while the male perches nearby. Kingbirds are fairly conspicuous about their nest location, look near beaver ponds—they will feed nearby, returning to its perch near the nest or bringing the food directly to the nest. Kingbirds establish a life-long nesting area. They return to the park in late April and leave in late August for their fall migration to South America.

TIP: Kingbirds are frequently seen in developed areas, such as resort areas. They are often found on electrical wires, or other places that afford a good view of the area.

SIZE: 5–6 inches

HABITAT: Lowland forests, upland shrublands, and deciduous forests

OCCURRENCE: Summer, common

IDENTIFICATION: Black eye, subtle facial pattern

WARBLING VIREO
Vireo gilvus

By sight, the small, 5½ inch warbling vireo is a plain bird. Its persistent singing, done mostly by the male and its hanging basket-like nest are two of its distinctive and attractive traits. This bird is found in open deciduous forests. Considered a "modern" bird, it avoids mature dense woods, which researchers suggest has contributed to its increase as humans have expanded their impact.

The sexes look alike and both incubate their eggs, unlike their relative the red-eyed vireo whose males who do not incubate. They are the size of a warbler, but plumper, deliberate in movement and known to eat harmful insects including caterpillars, moths, butterflies. They catch bugs like a flycatcher and pick insects off twigs and leaves. Warbling vireos are incessant singers with the male being the primary singer. He will sing continuously while on the nest. During the month of nesting, males and females change places frequently. The nests, similar to red-eyed vireos but are smaller and higher, look like hanging cups, the outside white from birch bark and white spider cocoons.

Warbling vireos are gray or olive gray, a light line over the eye, and white underparts that in fall turn to light yellow. Listen for them in open woodlands, groves of poplars, and clearings. Their song, sung mostly by the male, is a low-pitched, sweet rolling warble ending with an upward inflection. They are found singly or in pairs and are not as abundant as red-eyed vireos.

TIP: Listen for these birds on the Echo Bay Trail, the Tilson Creek Trail and on the Vermilion Gorge Trail and in the morning at Kabetogama Peninsula campsites.

SIZE: 5.5 – 6.5 inches
HABITAT: Lowland forests. upland shrublands , deciduous and coniferous forests
OCCURRENCE: Summer, common
IDENTIFICATION: Red eye, persistent song

RED-EYED VIREO
Vireo olivaceus

The red-eyed vireo is a small, grayish-green bird that is slightly larger than most warblers, 6 to 6½ inches in length. This bird is more often heard than seen as it calls over and over again short 3-note phrases, separated by brief pauses, "Here I am. Here I am. Where are you? Where are you?" For this constant repetition, it has been nicknamed "the Preacher."

The red-eyed vireo is the most common bird in the park and in Minnesota forests in general. It prefers mature forests, either deciduous or mixed upland types. Although it usually sings from near the top of trees, it nests within 10 feet of the ground. Vireos are a migratory species that nest in the park during the spring and summer, but they winter in South America.

This bird primarily feeds on insects and may contribute significantly to reducing populations of insects that cause disease problems in trees.

The red-eyed vireo can be distinguished from other vireos by its black-bordered white eyebrow stripe. It has no wing bars. It can be difficult to see the red eyes from a distance.

TIP: The red-eyed vireo is one of the few birds that tend to call repeatedly, even during hot afternoons. Listen for it on the Chain of Lakes Trail or the Cruiser Lake Trail. See T.S Roberts' chapter on this species for an interesting account. The red-eyed vireo is the "Wake Robin" of John Burroughs.

SIZE: 10 – 13 inches

HABITAT: Bog and coniferous forests

OCCURRENCE: Permanent, common

IDENTIFICATION: Resembles a large chickadee

GRAY JAY
Perisoreus canadensis

Gray jays are a common sight in northern coniferous forests. They are very curious and a bit brazen which has given them many nicknames such as, "grease bird," "camp robber," and "meat bird." Native Americans regard the jay with respect, and have given them the name "wiss-ka-tjon" which has evolved into the English name "whiskey-john." They tend to be quite fearless, and can swoop down in a campsite and retrieve either your lunch or a nearby mouse that was after your lunch. Either way, jays are resourceful and hearty, and viewed year round. The have a taste for berries, bird eggs, spiders, and seeds, and carrion and fat during the cold winter months. They are aptly named for their petty thievery, and for their tendency to stash their food in hollowed out stumps and woodpecker holes.

The gray jay is slightly bigger than a robin. Both sexes look alike, with long tails, short rounded wings, and pearl gray overall. The back of the head is a dark gray, with short whiskers at the base of its black bill, and brown eyes. They feel at home in fairly dense spruce and balsam forests, where they generally nest about five to ten feet high. Their nesting behavior starts early in the year, with mating behavior intensifying as nesting time nears. Gray jays mate for life, and will find a new mate only if one dies. Jays build their nests together, and often eggs are in nests while there is still snow on the ground.

TIP: In the spring, look for a family of gray jays at the beaver pond on the Chain of Lakes Trail or near Cruiser Lake.

SIZE: 12 inches

HABITAT: Deciduous and coniferous forests

OCCURRENCE: Permanent, common

IDENTIFICATION: Crested, powder blue bird with white belly

BLUE JAY
Cyanocitta cristata

This delightful blue bird with black stripes and white patches on its tail and wings is often heard before it is seen. They have a raucous, piercing "jay, jay, jay" call, and are most boisterous in the spring. They gently glide from tree to tree, and are about 11 inches in length. Blue jays don a beautiful crest and black necklace. Their underparts are a light gray. Males and females have similar behavior, and look identical.

Things quiet down in the woods after blue jays have paired. Now their focus has changed to building their nests. The males start several nests, but both males and females finish the work. The nests are built ten to twenty feet above the ground, and are made of twigs, bark, leaves, plastic, string, cloth, and paper. The male feeds the female during incubation, and both parents feed their young. The male continues to feed the female while the chicks are maturing. After the young leave the nest, the family travels together. Young blue jays often call to get food from their parents. With the onset of fall they gather in larger flocks.

Jays are quite bold, and seem to be quite social around humans, which gives us all a good chance to observe their behavior.

TIP: Blue jays can be found in nearly all woodland habitats, even in backyards and feeders.

SIZE: 17–21 inches
HABITAT: Deciduous and coniferous forests
OCCURRENCE: Summer, common
IDENTIFICATION: Medium-sized ebony bird

COMMON OR AMERICAN CROW
Corvus brachyrhynchos

Crows are considered one of the most intelligent birds, an argument used when looking at their adaptability and human inability to exterminate them. They are very sociable and easily recognized by their "caw" call. They are all black, and 17 to 21 inches in size. They can be found in Voyageurs but the park is on the northern edge of their range. Easily confused with the common raven, a common year-round resident to the boreal forest, their less loud "caw-caw" call and the fan-shaped tail distinguish them from the larger, hawk-size raven that has a guttural "wonk-wonk" call and a wedge-shaped tail. Given the similarities of the crow and the raven, concerns have been raised over a Minnesota crow hunting law and the difficulties in distinguishing the two.

Crows are omnivorous and have a high reproductive capacity, laying four to six eggs in a twig-stick nest lined with feathers and grass.

TIP: Look for crows along the water's edge, collected in trees and loudly socializing with each other.

SIZE: 21 – 27 inches

HABITAT: Deciduous and coniferous forests

OCCURRENCE: Permanent, common

IDENTIFICATION: Large ebony bird thick bill, deep voice

COMMON RAVEN
Corvus corax

The black raven, the largest of our perching birds (passerines), is a native of the wilderness boreal forest, which rings the Northern Hemisphere and includes Voyageurs National Park. This bird, credited in cultural lore for many creationist feats, is considered to be very intelligent and has been widely studied. The omnivorous raven is said to lead wolves to dead forest mammals, wait for them to open and eat most of the prey and then beat off the wolves with their wings to claim their finder's fee. Their summer diet is primarily berries, due to low carrion supplies.

Easily confused with the common crow, ravens are the largest of the corvidae family, with a wingspan of 4 to 4.5 feet. They require several hops before becoming airborne, whereas crows jump directly into the air. Given this family's penchant for being vocal, an easy way to determine the raven/crow distinction is to listen to their call. Crows 'caw' and ravens make a guttural croaking sound.

TIP: Starting in February, look for male ravens performing acrobatics such as death defying and spinning dives. While they are enjoying themselves, their diving skills also serve as a mating attraction. Look for ravens flying over the forest. They are much shier of human encroachment than crows. Listen for their call to determine if you are looking at a crow or a raven.

SIZE: 5–6 inches

HABITAT: Open water, lowland forests, upland shrublands

OCCURRENCE: Summer, common

IDENTIFICATION: Metallic blue above, white below

TREE SWALLOW
Tachycineta bicolor

It is a common sight in most of Minnesota to see a group of tree swallows twittering and looping over the surface of a calm lake and catching flying insects. They are also found in meadows and rural areas. Tree swallows are the first swallows to migrate north each spring; they do so in large colonies, and fly at speeds up to 25 miles per hour.

This species does not need to winter as far south as other swallows because they include some seeds and berries in their diet, the only North American swallows to regularly do so.

By far, however, the majority of their diet consists of insects: beetles, flies, ants, also bees and wasps. They nest in natural tree cavities, but will gladly settle down in man-made nest boxes.

Look for a sparrow-sized, triangular shaped bird, with shallow wing beats. They have a metallic blue to green dark back, and pure white underside. Their song is a trilly chatter.

TIP: Look for these birds at the water's edge as you walk the trails and paths around the Rainy Lake Visitor Center, Mica Bay, and Kettle Falls.

SIZE: 5–6 inches

HABITAT: Open water

OCCURRENCE: Summer, common

IDENTIFICATION: Buff rump, chestnut cheeks

CLIFF SWALLOW
Petrpchelidon pyrrhonota

This prolific species has taken advantage of the many sheltered sites like bridges and barns, thus becoming more and more widespread throughout the United States. They are small, fast flyers, and feed mostly on the wing. They are often seen in Voyageurs swooping down to the water in pursuit of flying insects like beetles, flies, winged ants, and bees.

Cliff swallows have pale rumps, glossy blue-black backs, brown necks, and long squared tails. They typically build their nests in colonies on the sides of rocky ledges or buildings. Their nest is made of dried mud shaped like a gourd with a small entrance on the side. Both parents build a new nest or repair a former nest, and they both feed their nestlings.

These are long distance migrants and winter in South America. The spring arrival of the cliff swallow in Capistrano, California, is celebrated every March 19, even though they actually appear in February.

TIP: Look for these fast flying birds in the air, around the Rainy Lake Visitor Center and in the Ash River Resort community.

SIZE: 6-7 inches
HABITAT: Open water
OCCURRENCE: Summer, common
IDENTIFICATION: Deeply forked tail

BARN SWALLOW
Hirundo rustica

Watch for these fast, electric blue backed birds as they dive and turn skill-fully through the air. Almost 7 inches long, they have a chestnut-colored throat and forehead, buff-colored underparts, and a deeply forked tail. They fly easily, showing their long outer tail feathers. The most widespread of all swallows they feed flying gracefully low to the ground or water in pursuit of flying insects. They have a dark band on their cinnamon-colored chest, and fly easily showing their long outer tail feathers.

Males arrive first in the park and pick a site for their nest. Courtship involves beautiful aerial chases, and when paired, the birds mate for life. They build their cup-like nest out of dried grasses and mud, and line them with feathers. These sites are developed in sheltered rocky crevices or often on buildings. Several pairs may nest in an area, but large colonies do not develop.

TIP: Look for these birds around park visitor centers and the business section of Crane Lake.

SIZE: 4.5 – 5.5 inches

HABITAT: Upland shrublands and deciduous forests

OCCURRENCE: Permanent, common

IDENTIFICATION: Gray with black cap and chin

BLACK-CAPPED CHICKADEE
Poecile atricapillus

This wonderful year-round friend is a small gray bird with a black cap, white cheeks, white wing coverts with secondaries edged in white. They are about warbler size, 4¾ to 5¾ inches in length, and very sociable.

These fluffy birds gather in small flocks during the winter, and pair up to defend their nesting sites by late winter. Males often feed their partners in the early spring. They nest in holes of trees, by enlarging an already rotted cavity, or use old woodpecker holes. The female generally builds the nest with a base of moss, and softer animal hair as the lining. They are very common in open woods and forest edges amongst birches, alders, and deciduous trees.

They eat mostly insects and seeds, but may fly out and hawk insects in midair. They can be seen "stashing" their find in tree bark crevices to recover later. Chickadees hop from branch to branch, and are often found hanging upside down to reach under limbs and branches. Their call is a cheery chick-a-dee-dee-dee, which can be heard in Voyageurs while walking the trails or cross-country skiing.

TIP: Look for a chickadee around your campsite or cabin.

SIZE: 4 inches

HABITAT: Coniferous forests

OCCURRENCE: Permanent, common

IDENTIFICATION: Black eye strip, chestnut belly

RED-BREASTED NUTHATCH
Sitta canadensis

This bird tends to travel headfirst down trunks in search of insects and spiders in the summer and conifer seeds in the winter. A small bird, 4½ inches in length, they are found throughout Canada and the United States. They have a blue-gray back, are rusty colored underneath, don a small dark cap, and white eye-stripe.

Their courtship calls are soft and musical. Males feed females during courtship, and they both excavate a rotted cavity for their nest. They nest in coniferous woods, feeding and often hoarding cone seeds. They may stay in the nesting area all year if the cone crop is good, and can store seeds from a heavily laden cone tree in their nest.

Usually they are fearless of humans, and you can hear their "tin horn"-like call which is a quiet "nyeep, nyeep." If cone crops are not plentiful, they may move further south, and take advantage of bird feeders.

TIP: Look for these birds on conifer trees along park trails, near campsites and in resort areas. A good tip to identify a nuthatch is watching them go headfirst down a tree as they pick at available insects.

SIZE: 4.5 – 5 inches

HABITAT: Upland shrublands

OCCURRENCE: Summer, common

IDENTIFICATION: Intricate song, cocks head back while singing

HOUSE WREN
Trogolodytes aedon

This friendly, little, plump, active bird was named long ago for its tendency to nest around people's homes, in birdhouses. In Voyageurs, you may find a nest in any kind of cavity or tree hollow. Males arrive first in the park, and often build several nests from which the female can choose. The female then puts her finishing touches of lining in the nest and lays 5 to 8 pinkish-white eggs. Both parents feed their nestlings. Wrens may leave the nest 12 to 18 days after they hatch, so parents often have two broods a year.

House wrens are grayish brown in color with a faint eyebrow. They are about 4¾ to 5 inches tall, and often bounce from branch to branch with their tails held up in the air. They have a rich bubbling song that cascades from a high to low pitch. When startled they make a scolding "churr" or buzzing sound. They can be aggressive to other hole-nesting species, and may destroy their eggs and young.

They arrive in the park shortly after the warblers arrive, and may well be the first to migrate south again.

TIP: You may find this inquisitive bird very low in dense vegetation, foraging actively for insects starting the end of May.

SIZE: 4 – 4.5 inches

HABITAT: Sedge fens

OCCURRENCE: Summer, uncommon

IDENTIFICATION: Intricate song, lives in marshes, cattails

SEDGE WREN
Cistothorus platensis

This busy little bird is about 4½ inches long and easier to hear than see. They have a brown and black striped crown and back, white eyebrows, and buff underparts. Their call is a few single notes followed by a dry trill or chatter, somewhat like the sound of an old fashioned sewing machine. They are hard to see as they creep around in damp sedge meadows or among other vegetation on the ground. They feed on a wide variety of insects.

Their nesting sites seem to be clearly established one year, but vacant the next. Like the house wren the male may build "dummy nests" for the females to choose from. Males may have more than one mate. The nests are built very low to the ground amid standing grasses and woven into a globular shape with grasses and plant down. Sedge wrens are very territorial, and may puncture the eggs of a nearby nest. Young wrens are fed by both parents, and leave the nest between 12 and 14 days after hatching.

TIP: Listen for the sedge wren as you walk the Oberholtzer Trail, the Echo Bay Trail or the Peninsula-based trails.

SIZE: 3.5 – 4 inches

HABITAT: Upland shrublands and coniferous forests

OCCURRENCE: Summer, uncommon

IDENTIFICATION: Tiny, yellow cap

GOLDEN-CROWNED KINGLET
Regulus satrapa

These lively little birds are often found in groups fluttering about in the treetops. They are very active and glean insects and larvae from the foliage. The golden-crowned kinglet is olive-green above with a pale breast, white wing bars, and a bright yellow-orange crown patch bordered with black in the females, and yellow in the males.

They are very tiny hearty birds, able to withstand very cold temperatures. They make their nests high in conifers. Both males and females assist in making a globular hanging nest with an opening on the top. The nest is made of moss, lichens, twigs, and leaves, and is lined with feathers and plant down. The male aggressively guards the nest, and the female lays between five and ten eggs. The male may feed the female during incubation, and then both will feed the nestlings.

These acrobatic birds can be seen upside down on branches foraging for food, and are one of the earliest spring arrivals at Voyageurs.

TIP: Look for these birds, spring through fall, as they flit through the trees and shrubs along park trails.

SIZE: 3.5 – 4.5 inches

HABITAT: Bogs and coniferous forests

OCCURRENCE: Summer, common

IDENTIFICATION: Tiny, flicks its wings, ruby crown not readily visible

RUBY-CROWNED KINGLET
Regulus calendula

In the spring these small birds flit from branch to branch gleaning insects from treetops and low brush. In the summer they are harder to spot in Voyageurs because they nest high in conifers. They are one of the smallest North American birds, around 3½ to 4 inches in length, with a wingspan of 6¾ to 7¼ inches. They flick their tails and chatter as they move about. Their call is surprisingly strong for their small size and carries a variety of tones.

The male is olive-gray above with an incomplete eye ring, and two white wing bars. Occasionally, if excited, he will puff up his ruby red crown, which makes him easy to identify. The female resembles the male, but is duller and has no crest.

During migration, ruby-crowned kinglets may be spotted with nuthatches, warblers and other birds. This bird mainly feeds on small insects and spiders, gleaning them from tree needles and the bark of trees. They also eat elderberries and seeds, and drink tree sap.

Ruby-crowned kinglets' summer home is in Voyageurs, where they make a small hanging nest made of moss, lichens, twigs, and bark. Males display their brilliant red crowns while courting; otherwise they are usually hidden. They commonly nest in spruce, firs, or pines anywhere from 3 to 80 feet from the ground.

TIP: Look for kinglets along the Echo Bay Trail, they are usually in thick second growth shrubbery in the fall and winter.

VEERY

Catharus fuscescens

The veery, 7¼ inches in length, is a member of the thrush family. It is common, but rarely seen in the boreal forests of the north country. The veery is another bird of the "deep" forest, often found in wetter areas such as those with alder and willows. The veery gets its name from its unique call which has a resonant quality described as "connected spirals in a uniformly descending line" in the classic *Birds of America* (T. Gilbert Pearson, Editor-in-Chief).

If seen, the veery is reddish-brown above, and whitish below, with faint spots on its breast. The eye-ring is barely noticeable, if at all. There is no rufous tail as in the hermit thrush.

Veerys nest on or near the ground and eat snails, insects and small fruits. These birds are neotropical migrants, wintering in the southern United States, Central and South America.

TIP: Listen for the unique song of the Veery as you walk near deep, wet forests in the park in the evening, or as you camp in quiet places on the Kabetogama Peninsula. The song is easily recognized, once pointed out, and usually comes from near the ground as opposed to from the treetops: a descending "Veery, veery, veery, veery. Veery, veery, veery, veery."

SIZE: 6.5–7.5 inches

HABITAT: Swamp and coniferous forests

OCCURRENCE: Summer, common

IDENTIFICATION: Gray-brown plummage, song

SWAINSON'S THRUSH
Catharus ustulatus

The Swainson's thrush, 7¼ inches in length, is often found in closed-canopy, black spruce–tamarack forests. Formerly called the olive-backed thrush, this bird was named for William Swainson, an English naturalist.

This is a shy, elusive bird, more often heard than seen. Although its song is more musical than the veery's, it is easily remembered as like the veery's but ascending rather than descending. It is usually heard from the treetops.

When seen, it is distinguished from its close relatives, the veery and hermit thrush, by its olive-brown upper parts and buff eye-ring. Its breast is often more spotted than that of the veery. The Swainson's thrush often nests in the crotch of trees several feet from the ground and eats mostly insects such as weevils, ants, and bees.

TIP: Listen for the beautiful song of the Swainson's thrush in early morning or evening as you are walking through deep conifer forests. Or listen from your tent in the early morning if you are camped near a wet forest on the Kabetogama Peninsula.

SIZE: 6.5 – 7.5 inches

HABITAT: Bog and swamp

OCCURRENCE: Summer, common

IDENTIFICATION: Spiraling song, flicks its tail

HERMIT THRUSH
Catharus guttatus

The hermit thrush is a relatively small, 6¾ inches in length, shy thrush that is most often found in the deep, swampy woods of the park. Typical habitat includes wet forests with black spruce or tamarack as the main components and a closed canopy. Like most thrushes, it is more often heard than seen and when seen, it is difficult to distinguish from its relatives in the thrush family.

The song of the hermit thrush can be easily identified as it has an ethereal, flute-like quality. The phrases are similar, and repeat each other at different pitches, but each phrase begins with a clear whistled note. It is truly one of the most beautiful sounds in the forest.

The hermit thrush, when seen, often looks nervous, twitching its tail and starting suddenly from the ground. These birds nest on or close to the ground and feed on insects, fruits, and berries.

Distinguishing features of this bird include a complete whitish eye-ring and a rufous tail, which contrasts to its brownish back. Like all of its nearby relatives found in the park, Swainson's thrush and veery, it has a whitish breast with dark spots.

The hermit thrush spends its winters in the southern United States.

TIP: In the late spring through mid-summer, during the quiet of early morning or evening, listen for the flutelike song of the hermit thrush. It can be found throughout the park in areas near wet coniferous forests.

SIZE: 9–11 inches

HABITAT: Upland shrublands

OCCURRENCE: Summer, common

IDENTIFICATION: Red breast, black head

AMERICAN ROBIN
Turdus migratorious

The robin or "Little Robin Red-breast" is the largest of four local thrushes, ranging from 9 to 11 inches in length. The male robin, one of spring's first songbirds, returns to the park in April, about two weeks before the female. Sometimes the first robin seen in the spring is a robin that most likely wintered nearby. The male sings "cheerily cheer-up cheerio," a song that announces his territory. As a rule of thumb, robins, grackles and flickers arrive at the same time in the park. In September and October, robins flock in open fields before migrating south.

Robins' diet consists of 40 percent insects and less than 60 percent vegetables and have a reputation for eating too many fruits and vegetables.

Robins prefer horizontal branches or forks in trees or shrubs as a base to build their nests. They also build nests in houses, barns and bridges. The female will have two to three broods a year, laying four "robins egg blue" eggs at a time. Robins are protective of their young and are known to dive-bomb intruders if they approach too close to the nest. The sexes look alike — bright red breasts on a dark gray body, but the males have a darker head.

TIP: Look for robins on the forest edge, feeding on ground insects, eating the sweet blueberries on high exposed Canadian Shield outcroppings and raspberries along the park's trails.

SIZE: 8–9 inches
HABITAT: Upland shrublands
OCCURRENCE: Summer, common
IDENTIFICATION: Gray body, black cap, cat call

GRAY CATBIRD
Dumetella carolinensis

These plain gray birds have a black cap and reddish-brown patch at the underside base of their tail. They may be plain but they have loads of personality. They make several different calls and harsh sounds while hiding in the shrubbery. Their calls range from "meow" to a slur call when they are alarmed, hence their name. They are also very good mimics.

Catbirds are about robin sized, 8½ inches long. They nest, breed, and feed in the same area. Males arrive first at nesting sites and use their "cat call" to advertise their territory. Males defend a smaller feeding territory after the females show up. Females arrive later and complete one of several nests started by the males. Their nests are found in low dense undergrowth bordering fields, lakes, or streams, and are similar to mockingbird nests. Busy foraging for insects in the spring, the male feeds the female while she guards the nest, and lays eggs. Females tend to stay closest to the nest and feed the young.

Later in the summer they feed on berries, and can often be seen out in the open expressively cocking their tails. These birds are delightful to watch and have been known to care for other birds that lay eggs in their nest.

TIP: Listen for their cat calls in the spring as you walk the Echo Bay Trail.

SIZE: 11.5 inches

HABITAT: Upland shrublands

OCCURRENCE: Summer, common

IDENTIFICATION: Cinnamon brown above, white below, yellow eye

BROWN THRASHER
Toxostoma rufum

Although most often seen as a blur between low-lying shrubs, the male brown thrasher can also be spotted atop trees giving spectacular vocal performances. The brown thrasher is a member of the mockingbird family, and, although theirs is not as elaborate as a mockingbird's song, they share the intricacies noted of this family's namesake. Brown thrashers will sing the songs of cardinals, flickers, thrushes, and others, along with their own song, likened to, "Hello? Hello? Yes, yes. Who is it? Who is it? I should say, I should say, how's that? How's that?" and also an alarm "smack!" Note that each song phrase is doubled.

It prefers low thickets in rural areas, pastures, and farms. It is often confused with thrushes, which it resembles, but is larger and has a longer tail. One of America's best known and loved songbirds, it is declining over much of its range for the usual reasons.

This is a robin-sized bird with cinnamon-brown upper parts, and white, heavily streaked underside. It has a long, curved dark bill, two white wing bars, and golden eyes with black pupils. Thrashers are often solitary and retiring.

TIP: Look for thrashers as you walk through the open portions of parks trails in early summer.

SIZE: 6.5 – 8 inches

HABITAT: Open water and upland shrublands

OCCURRENCE: Summer, common

IDENTIFICATION: Tan bird with black eye stripe, seen in flocks

CEDAR WAXWING
Bombycilla cedrorum

The cedar waxwing is seven inches long, just bigger than a house sparrow. They have a very marked appearance, from its defined black mask, greenish-yellow chest, fawn colored crest, head and back, yellow-tipped tail and its nomenclature trait "waxwing," found on its outer wing feathers that looks like red dipped wax. They are known for their soft voices and trilling soft call of "zeee, zeee, zeee."

These are very social birds, more often found in flocks than individually. They are one of the species that has become accustomed to human-modified landscapes and can be approached close enough to touch before flying off. Adults are known to stiffen in an upright position and "freeze." Another common activity is to perch, several in a row, passing a single berry back and forth, beak to beak, never consuming the berry.

Cedar waxwings are known for their consumption of berries and for deflowering fruit trees. Waxwings behave like flycatchers before the berries grow, flying out from a perch and catching insects, feeding these high protein insects to their young. They lay three to five eggs, in a nest of fine grasses, weeds, fibers, moss, and hair. The eggs hatch in late summer, leaving the young to develop their adult markings the following year. They can have two broods a year.

TIP: Look for waxwings in open areas of the woods, near bogs and streams where berry-bearing shrubs find enough sun to grow, like the Cruiser Lake and Mica Bay Trails.

SIZE: 4–5 inches

HABITAT: Upland shrublands

OCCURRENCE: Summer, common

IDENTIFICATION: Olive-yellow breast, gray back, somewhat shy

NASHVILLE WARBLER
Vermivora ruficapilla

The Nashville warbler is one of over 23 species of warblers found in the park. While many animals fell onto hard times as settlers cleared the towering forests of eastern North America to create farmland, the Nashville warbler benefited. It proliferates in weedy pastures, and is becoming yet more abundant as those same farms are now being abandoned and left to become overgrown.

In 1808, Alexander Wilson named this bird after he first discovered it in Nashville. They are also known as birch warblers, Nashville swamp warblers and in the Sierra Nevada range, Calaveras warblers. They nest on the ground, usually in bogs, at the base of a shrub or bush, though males perch in trees to sing. Their diet consists of tent caterpillars, grasshoppers, and various other insects.

Nashvilles are chickadee-sized birds. Breeding males are olive-colored with a yellow throat and underside, prominent white eye ring, chestnut crown, and no wing bars. Females and juveniles are similar but less colorful.

TIP: Look for these birds in the wet, boggy, open areas of the Chain of Lakes and Cruiser Lake trails.

SIZE: 4.5–5 inches
HABITAT: Open water and upland shrublands
OCCURRENCE: Summer, common
IDENTIFICATION: No other bird seems this completely yellow

YELLOW WARBLER
Dendroica petechia

This familiar bird is a symbol of spring's arrival, and has the greatest range of all North American wood warblers. Yellow warblers may be seen in a variety of habitats while on migration, even in vast metropolitan areas. They favor the borders of small streams, but will nest and summer in gardens, parks, forests, prairies, and mountains, occupying any habitat that has small shrubs.

Yellow warblers eat, and feed their young, a number of destructive insects, including cankerworms, gypsy moth larvae, and bark beetles.

The female usually builds the nest, although closely monitored by the male, and behaves tame enough to allow observation. Unfortunately, it sometimes attracts the wrong kind of attention. The parasitic brown-headed cowbird is more often than not watching, and yellow warblers are one of the most frequent victims of cowbird parasitism. However, some females react in an unusual way. If they notice a cowbird egg in their nest, they simply build a new nest on top of it, and lay more eggs.

This is the only bird in North America that looks completely yellow from a distance. The male has a bright yellow head and underside, chestnut streaks on the breast, and its back is olive-yellow. Female and sub-adults are similar but duller.

TIP: Look for these warblers along the Oberholtzer Trail or on any of the Peninsula trails, particularly near beaver dams.

SIZE: 5 inches

HABITAT: Lowland forests

OCCURENCE: Summer, common

IDENTIFICATION: Yellow cap, chestnut flanks, song

CHESTNUT-SIDED WARBLER
Dendroica pensylvanica

This small warbler of about 5 inches in length reflects a colorful combination of a yellow cap, black mask, with white face, chin, chest, and belly. They have two yellow wing bars, and their sides are flanked with a beautiful chestnut color, hence their name. They prefer feeding in open aspen forests and at forest edges. Their whimsical whistle of "please please pleased to meetcha" can be heard throughout the forest, especially in the spring.

TIP: On a day in mid-May, before the trees leaf out, look for these colorful characters flitting about. They remain in the park throughout the summer.

SIZE: 5 inches
HABITAT: Upland shrublands and coniferous forests
OCCURRENCE: Summer, uncommon
IDENTIFICATION: Yellow breast with black stripes, white eyebrow

MAGNOLIA WARBLER
Dendroica magnolia

There are a handful of American wood warblers that share the characteristics of having a gray back with variations of black, white, and yellow mottled patterns about their bodies. Of all of them, the magnolia warbler is perhaps the most esthetically pleasing.

Observed in 1810 in magnolia trees, in Mississippi, by Alexander Wilson, they were named accordingly. They were, however, only en route to their breeding grounds in the northern coniferous forests, and do not have any particular relationship with Magnolia Trees at that latitude.

These beautiful birds are numerous, and on migration, often fill entire trees. Foraging on insects of all sorts, they may even be seen in orchards and gardens, low to the ground. Their song has been likened to "she knew she was right, yes, she knew she was right...pretty pretty Rachel."

This warbler is a chickadee-sized bird. The breeding male has a dark back, yellow rump, white wing patches, black raccoon mask with white eyebrows, and yellow underside with prominent black striping. Females, winter adults, and juveniles have gray backs with yellow undersides, and a white wing patch.

TIP: Visit the park in mid- to late-May and hike the Blind Ash Bay, Echo Bay, Chain of Lakes and Oberholtzer trails.

SIZE: 5–6 inches

HABITAT: Bogs

OCCURRENCE: Summer, common

IDENTIFICATION: Olive gray, yellow rump and cap

YELLOW-RUMPED WARBLER
Dendroica coronata

The yellow-rumped warbler was at one time divided into two separate species (the eastern myrtle warbler and western Audubon's warbler). However, in 1973, it was discovered that the two hybridize where their ranges overlap and that in fact, they are geographic representatives of one bird. The visitors to Voyageurs would be considered myrtle warblers.

Abundant and well known, the yellow-rumped warbler is one of our earliest spring migrants and it sometimes winters in North America. It travels north in waves; the males arrive shortly before the females. Diet consists mainly of insects, but it can also survive on berries and vegetation (one of the few warblers that can). Somewhat tame, yellow-rumps seem to get much closer to people than other warblers will. They nest in spruce-tamarack bogs.

An active chickadee-sized bird, foraging at mid to lower levels of trees and shrubs. In the spring, adult males are gray, with black streaks and chest, white throat, black "raccoon" mask, and yellow patches on sides, crown and rump. They have two white wing bars. Females, juveniles, and fall males are similar but much less colorful.

TIP: Look for these warblers on the bog walk at Orr and the DNR Ash River Trail. Wear boots and bug repellent for this trail.

SIZE: 5 inches

HABITAT: Lowland and deciduous forests

OCCURRENCE: Summer, uncommon

IDENTIFICATION: Yellow face, black throat

BLACK-THROATED GREEN WARBLER
Dendroica virens

Said to be one of the easiest warbler songs to learn, the black-throated green warbler's carol resembles the sound of "trees-trees-murmuring-trees." The caroler, however, usually remains well hidden, while singing, at the tops of trees.

This bird is usually observed during the migration season, while still en route to its northern breeding grounds of large pines and hemlocks. During the migration, the birds must eat voraciously to sustain their journey, and feed at any level of the forest, but often near the ground during late spring.

This warbler is a small bird with yellow cheeks and throat. The male has black above its breast. Its underside is white with olive above, streaked with black. They have two white wing bars.

The nest is constructed on a horizontal branch of a tree, up to 80 feet in the air, but usually lower. It is an orderly construction of vegetation held together with spider webs and lined with hair and feathers. Four to five eggs are laid and incubated for about twelve days. Both parents care for the young.

TIP: Look for them on the park's trails in May when they spend several weeks here before migrating north.

SIZE: 5.5 inches

HABITAT: Lowland deciduous and coniferous forests

OCCURRENCE: Transient, uncommon

IDENTIFICATION: Blackcapped, streaked flanks

BLACKPOLL WARBLER
Dendroica striata

Each spring, blackpoll warblers set out from South America to undertake the extraordinary task of crossing the Caribbean Sea to reach North America. They travel in groups by night, as all wood warblers do. Once they arrive in North America, they are subject to the hazards of colliding with tall buildings or lighthouses on their journey to northern Canada and Alaska, where their breeding range covers an extensive portion of the continent. Their fall flight over the Atlantic is even more spectacular.

Most are seen in the tops of tall trees, foraging for insects that have infested the branches and leaves, such as aphids or scales.

Blackpoll warblers are chickadee-sized birds. The breeding male has a distinct black cap, white belly, black and gray checkered body, and yellow legs. Females and juveniles are olive green. Both male and female have white wing bars.

TIP: Look for them the last three weeks in May on the Echo Bay Trail, the Peninsula trails and the Oberholtzer Trail.

SIZE: 5 inches

HABITAT: Deciduous forests

OCCURRENCE: Summer, common

IDENTIFICATION: Boldly striped, clings to trees like a woodpecker

BLACK-AND-WHITE WARBLER
Mniotilta varia

Black-and-white warblers are most often found creeping along branches and trunks of trees, carefully inspecting the bark for ants, flies, caterpillars, beetles, or spiders. They arrive at their nesting grounds in early spring, and are common in mixed deciduous forests all summer long. As the male hunts from tree to tree he sings his song: a trebly "wesee, wesee, wesee, wesee."

The male is striped length-wise black and white. Its undersides are white and it has a white eye stripe below and above the eye. The female is similar, but duller with a white belly.

The bill of a black-and-white warbler is slightly curved, unlike other warblers, and is somewhat similar to that of a creeper, which is how black-and-white warblers earned their nicknames "black-and-white creeper," and "pied creeper." However, unlike creepers, which move only up a tree, black-and-white warblers can scramble in any direction, somewhat like a nuthatch.

The nest is usually built on the ground, at the base of a tree or bush, or in the cavity in the top of a tree stump. The female lays four or five eggs, which she incubates for up to twelve days.

TIP: Look for this bird along the Echo Bay, Vermillion Gorge, and Oberholtzer Trails.

SIZE: 4.5 – 5.5 inches

HABITAT: Open water and upland shrublands

OCCURRENCE: Summer, common

IDENTIFICATION: Blackback, orange wing stripe, fans tail

AMERICAN REDSTART
Setophaga ruticilla

Known as "mariposas" (butterflies) in their wintering grounds of Central and South America, the American redstart is one of our most abundant warblers, as it favors second-growth woodland. "Redstart" is an interpretation of the Old-German "rothstert," which means "red-tail." Its diet consists almost exclusively of forest insects, and it nests from May to July in North America. The American redstart is among the most common victims of cowbird parasitism.

This is a chickadee-sized bird, active and fluttery, often taking flight to catch an insect and returning to the same perch. Redstarts have a habit of tipping forward and fanning out their tails to reveal colorful patterns. Adult males are glossy black with orange patches on their wings, tail, and sides. They have white bellies. Females are similar, but gray and orange.

TIP: Look for redstarts in shrubs on the forest's edge, next to the beaver ponds off of the Ash River Trail and on the Cruiser Lake Trail.

SIZE: 6 inches

HABITAT: Deciduous and coniferous forests

OCCURRENCE: Summer, common

IDENTIFICATION: Buff crown, song

OVENBIRD
Seiurus aurocapillus

The ovenbird is a shy little bird of deep forests, 6¼ inches in length, more often heard than seen. Through mid-July, it can be heard calling over and over again, "Teacher, Teacher, Teacher," in mature forests. Although their calls are often heard from the trees above, ovenbirds actually nest on the ground, making a small inconspicuous nest in the leaf litter. More often than not, the nest is slightly covered like a Dutch oven — hence, its name.

Ovenbirds have relatively plain, olive-green upperparts, and whitish underparts streaked with black. Their head is distinguished by a black stripe on either side of the crown; their eyes are surrounded by a whitish eye ring.

Ovenbirds, when seen, are usually walking (not hopping) on the ground or on a low branch. They characteristically bob their tails. Typical foods include caterpillars, especially tent caterpillars, cankerworms, and earthworms. These neotropical birds are the second most common bird in the park (the red-eyed vireo being most common).

TIP: Ovenbirds are one of the few birds who continue to call all afternoon, especially on hot humid days in June and July. Listen for the emphatic "Teacher, Teacher, Teacher" as you hike the Chain of Lakes Trail or any other inland trail in a mature forest.

Ovenbirds in Minnesota are associated with mature forests. According to studies, 50 percent of Minnesota's original forests were mature. Today, 4 percent of our forests statewide are considered "old growth." VNP plays an important role in protecting this type of habitat for northern songbirds.

SIZE: 5–5.5 inches

HABITAT: Bogs

OCCURRENCE: Summer, uncommon

IDENTIFICATION: Shy, gray head, olive belly

CONNECTICUT WARBLER
Oporornis agilis

Seldom seen and rarely even in Connecticut, this shy warbler was named by Alexander Wilson while traveling through New England in 1812. It then virtually disappeared from records for another seventy years, until 1883, when another ornithologist, Ernest Thompson Seton, found a nest in Manitoba, Canada.

The best way to find the Connecticut warbler is to listen for the male's frequent song, "beecher, beecher, beecher," as it is secretive and travels low, through scrub. It migrates north into southern Canada, northern Minnesota and Michigan's Upper Peninsula, favoring spruce-tamarack bogs for nesting. It feeds by walking along branches near the ground, foraging for insects and spiders in crevices of bark, or on the ground.

This is a chickadee-sized bird. Breeding males are gray-olive, with bluish-gray throat, a yellow underbelly, a prominent, full, white eye ring, and no wing bars. Females and juveniles are similar but duller, and also stay close to the ground.

TIP: Look for Connecticut warblers along the wetter portions of the park's trails, the bog walk at Orr and the DNR Ash River Trail, where boots and bug repellent are a good idea.

SIZE: 5.5 inches

HABITAT: Upland shrublands

OCCURRENCE: Summer, common

IDENTIFICATION: Dark head, olive yellow body

MOURNING WARBLER
Oporornis philadelphia

The Mourning warbler is the eastern counterpart to MacGillivray's warbler, which it closely resembles. Secretive and more often heard than seen, it forages in dense thickets and brambles for insects and spiders. The small, black bib adorning the warbler's neck suggested to Alexander Wilson the garb of a mourner. He recorded it as that in 1810, in Philadelphia (hence its Latin species name, although it is less common there than in southeast and central Canada, and the Great Lakes region).

Mourning warblers build their nests on or near the ground in ferns or goldenrod. They usually lay four white and brown speckled eggs. The eggs incubate in about twelve days and the young leave the nest when they are seven to ten days old.

Mourning warblers are chickadee-sized birds. Breeding males have blue-gray heads, with a black bib, yellow belly and olive-gray back. Females and juveniles are similar but duller. Females have no bib but pink legs.

TIP: Look for these birds on the Echo Bay Trail and the Blind Ash Bay Trail in early spring.

SIZE: 7.5 inches
HABITAT: Deciduous forests
OCCURRENCE: Summer, common
IDENTIFICATION: Only red bird with black wings

SCARLET TANAGER
Piranga olivacea

For every major forest region in North America, there is a different member of the tanager family. The scarlet tanager nests in northern and eastern deciduous forests. The black-winged and otherwise bright red male being one of our most vibrantly colored passerines, it is, oddly enough, rather inconspicuous and hard to see, as it forages slowly in the canopy of the forest, feeding on a variety of insects.

The males arrive from South America on their breeding territory before the females do, and can be heard high in the treetops caroling a nasal "quer-it, queer, queery...querit, queer." The females then arrive and choose a mate on the basis of song, after which the males court them by displaying their scarlet back from a low perch.

After the eggs are laid, the female incubates for thirteen or fourteen days. Once hatched the chicks remain in the nest for nine to fifteen days.

At the end of the summer, the males molt their gorgeous breeding plumage, which is then replaced by an olive-yellow coat, though his wings remain black. Identifying the male is unmistakable. No other Northern American bird has combination of bright red body with black wings and tail. Females, youths, and winter males are an olive-yellow with dark wings and tails, and gray beak.

TIP: Look for these birds as you hike through the park trails. Listen for their call and look for the colorful male. They have also been seen in resorts and campgrounds.

93

SIZE: 5.5 – 6.5 inches

HABITAT: Lowland forests and upland shrublands

OCCURRENCE: Summer, uncommon

IDENTIFICATION: Rufous cap, breast spot

AMERICAN TREE SPARROW
Spizella arborea

A cold climate bird, able to withstand harsh temperatures down to 28 degrees below zero, the American tree sparrow is a winter visitor to the contiguous United States. They arrive in flocks of thirty to forty birds, after which small subgroups of four to eight break off and travel together all winter long.

The common title "tree sparrow" and the Latin "arborea" are, actually, not very fitting. The birds spend little time in trees; instead they hop and scratch in the snow, where they find a variety of seeds, which make up the majority of their diet.

When spring comes to the United States, the tree sparrows begin their journey back to their northern nesting grounds, to which they fly up to three thousand miles. Upon arrival, the birds soon pair off and the male begins to sing his song to defend the couple's nesting territory. The female lays up to six eggs, which she incubates for twelve to thirteen days. The young leave the nest before they are able to fly.

Look for an average sparrow-sized bird with sexes outwardly alike. They have a rufous crown and eye line, with gray cheeks and eye stripe, white belly with dark brown spot on breast, with gray nape and sides, browning wings and tail. The upper mandible is dark, lowers yellow. They have two white wing bars on each wing.

TIP: During the winter months, look for these birds in frozen grassy areas of Tom Cod Bay, the west end of Sullivan Bay.

SIZE: 5 – 5.5 inches

HABITAT: Lowland forests and deciduous forests

OCCURRENCE: Summer, common

IDENTIFICATION: "sewing machine" song, rufous cap

CHIPPING SPARROW
Spizella passerina

The chipping sparrow has been referred to as our most domestic North American sparrow. When spring arrives they can be found in orchards, gardens, yards, fields and woodlands. In the past they would make their nests with horse hair, but with the decline of farming in America, they now use any hair they can find (it is said they will pull hair from a sleeping dog). Small and relatively tame, they have been known to eat seeds from human hands.

Once they have arrived on their nesting grounds, the males begin to sing their song, which is the basis of their common name. The song has been likened to the sound of a sewing machine, a series of monotonous chip notes. Sometimes the song is delivered slowly, other times it is sung so fast that it seems to be a continuous note. Chipping sparrows are known to sing both day and night.

First-winter birds lack the rufous crown of mature birds, and are notably smaller than adults.

Chipping sparrows are small sparrows with sexes outwardly alike. Adults have a rufous crown, white eye stripe, and black eye line which extends from the bill to the back of the head, as wells as white throat, gray belly, and drab brown backs. The tail is long and forked.

TIP: In the spring, walk the forest trails in Voyageurs and listen for their sewing machine-like song.

CLAY-COLORED SPARROW
Spizella pallida

The clay-colored sparrow is one of the harder sparrows to identify, as it looks much like an eastern counterpart, the immature chipping sparrow, and like the western Brewer's sparrow (not found in Voyageurs National Park). The clay-colored sparrow can be found in dry, bushy plains during summer. Hybrids have been reported of both clay-colored and chipping sparrows, and of clay-colored and Brewer's sparrows, where their nesting territories meet, as all three species prefer the same type of habitat.

Flying by day and night from its wintering grounds in Mexico, the clay-colored sparrow arrives at its nesting grounds in Northern America in May. The male then claims up to one acre of territory, which he announces by singing his song, "zee-zee-zee," from a low-lying shrub or fence post. The clay-colored sparrow is one of the few northern prairie birds that continues to sing its song well into the heat of July.

This is an average sparrow-sized bird with sexes outwardly alike. They have sharply outlined brown ear patches, with white eye line, pale gray patch down the center of head, and a white stripe on each side of the throat. They have a buff-gray breast and belly, two white bars on each wing, gray nape, and flesh colored legs and bill.

TIP: Look for these birds in open fields of park trails including the DNR's Ash River trail lower loop system and the end of the Echo Bay trail.

SIZE: 5.5 – 6 inches

HABITAT: Lowland forests and upland shrublands.

OCCURRENCE: Summer, common

IDENTIFICATION: Streaked, notched bill

SAVANNAH SPARROW
Passerculus sandwichensis

The Savannah sparrow was given its common name in honor of the city of Savannah, Georgia, where naturalist Alexander Wilson first discovered it in 1811. It is abundant and widespread, nesting wherever grasslands join wetlands in nearly all of North America. It is, however, quite secretive, and if disturbed it tends to run away like a mouse through the grass rather than take flight and disclose its whereabouts.

The female almost always builds the nest in a natural hollow or one dug out by the bird. It is well hidden by the grassy environment which the Savannah sparrow frequents, and sometimes the birds form loose colonies in particular areas. Four to five variably colored eggs are laid, which hatch in twelve days, being incubated by both parents. The brood leaves the nest after about fourteen days.

This is an average-sized sparrow with sexes outwardly similar. It resembles the song sparrow, with small patch on its stripped chest, but it has a smaller tail. It is mottled brown with white streaks and a yellow patch above its eye in nesting season. Legs are flesh-colored.

TIP: Look for this bird as you walk through the damp and open parts of the park's trails.

SIZE: 5 inches
HABITAT: Upland shrublands
OCCURRENCE: Summer, uncommon
IDENTIFICATION: Orange head stripes

LE CONTE'S SPARROW
Ammodramus leconteii

Nesting in North Central America, Le Conte's sparrow is extremely hard to observe, as it will not flush from the grasslands it inhabits, but instead drops to the ground where it is well hidden by the tall grass. Like the Savannah sparrow, it usually runs away on the ground, as opposed to flying.

This small sparrow was named in honor of John L. Le Conte, a physician in Philadelphia who was a friend of John James Audubon and an early American naturalist.

The Le Conte's sparrow arrives from the southern United States on its nesting grounds in April or May. The male sings his song, which sounds like an insect, "z-z-z- buzzzz," atop a long grass stem. The song lasts for about one second, and is higher pitched than the similar song of the Savannah sparrow, with which it often shares nesting grounds. The female usually lays four gray-ish white speckled eggs, which she incubates for twelve to thirteen days. How long the young stay in the nest after hatching is still a mystery.

This is a small sparrow with sexes outwardly alike. It has brown wings, yellowish orange throat and eye streak, gray cheek, white belly, and pink legs and bill.

TIP: To find this bird, look out over the grassy areas along the Oberholtzer Trail and the Echo Bay Trail.

SIZE: 6 – 7.5 inches

HABITAT: Open water, upland shrublands, deciduous forests

OCCURRENCE: Transient, uncommon

IDENTIFICATION: Large sparrow, rufous plumage

FOX SPARROW
Passerella iliaca

Nesting in upper North America, and wintering in the southern United States, the fox sparrow is only likely to be encountered in the park during migration. Fortunately, this is when it is most observable, for it sings vibrantly and flute-like while it travels, and it nests in such thick cover it is hard to find once it reaches its breeding territory. One of North America's largest sparrows, it is often confused with the hermit thrush.

Look for a large sparrow. The sexes are outwardly alike with a heavily streaked white underside and a tawny rufous upperside and tail. They have a gray eye stripe and nape, with a rufous cheek, yellow lower and dark upper mandible.

TIP: Take a trip to the park in mid to late May and listen for its song on any of the park trails.

SONG SPARROW
Melospiza melodia

One of our most familiar songbirds, the song sparrow has a range that covers nearly the entire North American continent. Those that nest in the far north come south in the winter. This abundant bird often lives close to people, who have given it a variety of nicknames ranging from "everybody's darling" to "swamp bird," and its melodious song is often a sure sign of the arrival of spring. Naturalist Henry David Thoreau likened the trill of the song sparrow to, "Maids, Maids, hang up your teakettles, ettle, ettle, ettle."

The song sparrow is regularly parasitized by cowbirds; in Mexico City, in 1953, over fifty percent of the nests had been invaded. Yet, song sparrows still thrive, with some banded birds reaching the age of ten years old. There are thirty-one known subspecies, from small, pale desert birds, to large brown Alaskan ones.

Females build the nests and sometimes raise three broods per year. Diet consists of insects and seeds in the summer, and berries and seeds in the winter. It will frequent bird feeders.

Look for an average sparrow-sized bird with the sexes similar, a tan, mottled back, wings and tail, a gray and brown streaked head, white breast and belly with heavy dark brown breast streaks, and a diagnostic dark brown "heart shaped" patch in the center of its breast. They pump their tails in flight.

TIP: Listen for the song sparrow, during its mating season, as you hike the park trails starting the end of May through mid-summer.

SIZE: 5 inches

HABITAT: Bogs, swamps, fens, marshes, and open water

OCCURRENCE: Summer, common

IDENTIFICATION: Tan wings, dark rufous cap

SWAMP SPARROW
Melospiza georgiana

This close relative of the song sparrow favors swamps, damp meadows, bogs, and slow moving streams in its summer territory of northeastern America and northern Canada. However, during migration and on its wintering grounds of southeastern America, it is likely to be encountered in a wider variety of habitats.

While in its wetland nesting territory, it feeds by wading in shallow water and catching insects such as beetles, ants, grasshoppers, and crickets. The male sings from the top of a cattail or in the branches of willows a musical metallic "weet-weet-weet-weet." It readily responds to imitations or squeaking sounds, which is a good way to get the bird to come into view.

The nest is built among cattails, usually by the female, who lays four to five pale green, speckled eggs, which hatch twelve to fifteen days later. The young leave the nest after twelve to thirteen days, but occasionally fall into the water and fall victim to turtles, frogs, or fish.

Look for an average sparrow-sized bird; sexes outwardly alike; dark, with rusty cap and white throat, flesh-colored legs, and dark bill. It has a tan cheek and eye line, gray eye stripe and nape, gray wash on chest, and tan flanks. Individuals may show a rusty spot in the center of their breast.

TIP: Look for these birds in the boggy, swampy sections of the Peninsula trails and the wetter sections of the Oberholtzer Trail.

SIZE: 6–7 inches

HABITAT: Lowland forests, upland shrublands, deciduous and coniferous forests

OCCURRENCE: Summer, common

IDENTIFICATION: Yellow eyespot, striped face, song

WHITE-THROATED SPARROW
Zonotrichia albicollis

In spring, when one is hiking through the variety of habitats Voyageurs offers, the song of this abundant sparrow rings from many different directions at the same time; at different pitches and tempos according to each individual bird. It is the males that do the majority of the singing. "Old Sam Peabody-Peabody-Peabody" becomes a mantra of the north woods in the early breeding season, and can be heard both day and night.

The white-throated sparrow nests as far north as the trees will allow, and is itself characteristic of the Canadian wilderness. It winters in the southern United States, and is quite common in urban and residential areas during migration. It feeds mainly on the ground, mostly on grass and weed seeds, but will also eat insects. The nests are built by females, low to or on the ground and well concealed.

The sexes are similar with rusty brown mottled back and wings and two white wing bars. They have alternating black and white stripes on their head with a bright yellow "eyebrow," white chin, gray breast, and white flanks.

TIP: Listen for their song in the spring on any of the park's trails.

SIZE: 6–7.5 inches

HABITAT: Lowland forests and upland shrublands

OCCURRENCE: Transient, uncommon

IDENTIFICATION: Bold black and white cap, pinkish bill

WHITE-CROWNED SPARROW
Zonotrichia leucophrys

More abundant in the west than the east, the white-crowned sparrow may be seen in Voyageurs National Park during migration, often mixed into flocks of white-throated sparrows (to which it is closely related). This bird has been a staple for scientists attempting to unlock the secrets of bird migration; much of what we know about migration has been discovered in their experiments.

The song begins very similar to the white-throated sparrow; a clear whistle, but this is followed by a somber "more wet, wetter, chee-zee." It hops about in the grass and scratches with both feet in search of food: mosses, willow catkins, and a variety of insects.

The sexes are similar with bold black and white streaks on their crown, a lustrous gray face, neck and breast, white throat and belly, and a mottled brown back, rump, wings, and tail. They have two white wing bars. Juveniles are similar but duller.

TIP: Look for this bird along the Oberholtzer Trail and the Chain of Lakes Trail in May.

SIZE: 5–6.5 inches

HABITAT: Bogs, lowland forests, upland shrublands, and coniferous forests

OCCURRENCE: Transient, common

IDENTIFICATION: Gray plumage, pink bill, flocks

DARK-EYED (SLATE-COLORED OR NORTHERN) JUNCO
Junco hyemalis

The "slate-colored" junco is a member of a genus of finches that were, until 1973, considered to be several separate species. They are now grouped together as the single species the dark-eyed junco; as it was found that they interbred and were actually geographic subspecies of the same bird. Our "slate-colored" junco is the nominate (first named) subspecies, and the only junco usually encountered east of the Mississippi River.

Seemingly just as at home at fifteen degrees below zero as at sixty above, the hardy junco is a welcome sight as it arrives in fall from its breeding grounds in Alaska and Canada. It is common at feeders in wintertime, picking up seeds that fall to the ground. Small family groups return to the same place each winter.

In summer, juncos eat insects of all sorts, and in winter tend to feed on seeds and winter berries. Nests are built by females in a variety of places, from low-lying bushes and small trees, to beneath ledges on houses, and in discarded cans.

Look for a sparrow-sized gray bird, with a white belly, bright pink beak and legs, and dark eyes. Immature birds are speckled brown. Its song is a musical trill and it has an alarm chirp.

TIP: Look for these birds in the fall and winter in resort areas that are known to have bird feeders. Look also on the edges of bogs and conifer stands where they will feed on the ground and perch in the trees.

SIZE: 8 inches
HABITAT: Deciduous forests
OCCURRENCE: Summer, common
IDENTIFICATION: Male, black and white with red breast, thick bill, drab female

ROSE-BREASTED GROSBEAK
Pheucticus ludovicianus

These large finches are sometimes hard to see but their beautiful robin-like whistles are clear and melodious and heard throughout the spring and summer. You may spy one perched on a high dead branch and notice a bright red splotch of color on its breast. They stand about 7¼ inches high. They have black heads, large tails, and white wing bars, white underneath, with a white rump. Their pale-colored cone-shaped bill is very distinctive, as well as their red wing linings which show when in flight.

Grosbeaks breed in open deciduous woods. The nest is built typically by the female who will use twigs, weeds, leaves, and sometimes animal hair. The nest is sometimes so flimsy that you can see the eggs from below. They are found 5 to 20 feet up in the branches.

Grosbeaks primarily eat insects but do eat some fruit, seeds, and flowers. They usually migrate late in spring, and early in the fall. Their numbers seem to be stable in Voyageurs.

TIP: Take a walk through the Echo Bay Trail or the Vermilion Gorge trail in the spring and summer when looking for this bird. Listen for their call and, using a good pair of binoculars, you should be able to find this beautiful, large finch.

SIZE: 7–9.5 inches

HABITAT: Marshes, open water marshes, and open water

OCCURRENCE: Summer, common

IDENTIFICATION: Red and yellow shoulder patch, camouflaged female

RED-WINGED BLACKBIRD
Agelaius phoeniceus

As you near a marsh setting and you hear the welcoming song, "O-ka-LEEEE" you will know that you are in the habitat of the red-winged blackbird. The red-winged blackbird is primarily a marsh bird but can be found in different water settings. A typical way to find these birds is in the spring, when you can spot the male, with its red shoulder patches, perched high on a cattail—singing.

Based on their physical traits and the quality of the marsh that has been secured by the male, a female will decide with whom to mate. Due to their adaptive personality, they are considered by some the most populous birds in North America. Studies suggest that this bird was not originally a water area bird. For example, its coloring does not fit the marshland habitat colors.

They make their nest in the marsh using strips of cattail leaves. A pair of blackbirds will raise 2-3 broods a year, using different nests for each brood.

TIP: Hike the Chain of Lakes, Ash River beaver pond overlook or Cruiser Lake trails where marshes and beaver ponds are common. The trail to the Beaver Pond, across from the Rainy Lake Visitor Center on Black Bay is another good choice.

SIZE: 12 inches
HABITAT: Upland shrublands, deciduous and coniferous forests
OCCURRENCE: Summer, common
IDENTIFICATION: Dark metallic plummage

COMMON GRACKLE
Quiscalus quiscula

This is a commonly found black bird. The male has an iridescent purplish body and is about the size of a blue jay. They arrive in the park in early spring with the return of robins and flickers and depart late in the fall. They have an extremely varied diet and are reported to use their bill to kill house sparrows and mice. They are known to be numerous and noisy near dwellings, public gatherings, and bird feeders.

Grackles nest in conifers and have one brood a year, hatching five eggs that are pale blue with brown blotches. They are omnivorous, known to eat a variety of insects, frogs, lizards, small birds, and bird eggs. They will steal worms from robins as they pull them from the ground. They nest and roost in colonies and are known for being both loud in flocks and generally gregarious. Kestrels attack grackles as a food source.

TIP: Look for grackles roosting in flocks in conifers on the edge of the forest and sitting on the ground in open spaces.

SIZE: 6–8 inches

HABITAT: Deciduous and coniferous forests

OCCURRENCE: Summer, Common

IDENTIFICATION: Blackbird with brown head

BROWN-HEADED COWBIRD
Molothrus ater

It has been hypothesized that this bird, rather infamous for its parasitic method of rearing its young, once roamed America's grasslands with the vast herds of bison. In keeping up with the bison's migration, they hadn't time to stop and build a nest in which to raise their young, so they deposited their eggs in the nests of other birds, leaving a different species with the full responsibility of raising the young cowbirds. However, as the bison were decimated, the birds simply moved into pastureland and became associated with domestic cows. Another theory is that cowbirds simply lost their will to defend a territory for reproduction, and stopped building nests (Friedman 1929). Cowbirds are the only birds in North America completely dependent on other species to raise their young; they are obligatory parasites.

The female lays up to 10 or 12 eggs per season, and the hosts incubate the eggs for roughly 11 days. Cowbirds eat many insects, particularly grasshoppers, but mainly they eat seeds and fruits.

Look for males that are a medium robin-sized blackbird with brown head. Females are similarly sized but uniformly gray. Their song is a gurgling "glug-glug-glee." They are found in a variety of habitats: urban, pastoral, and woodlands.

TIP: Look for Cowbirds in open areas of the Echo Bay Trail and trails of the Ash River Road. They are often seen in grassy fields or adjacent woodlands. Watch for them where you find their "victims" (largely warblers) during the breeding season.

BALTIMORE ORIOLE
Icterus galbula

This beautifully brilliant colored songbird is a delight to experience. Formerly, this oriole was divided into the Baltimore and Bullock's oriole. The two have been combined to into the species first called the northern oriole, now renamed the Baltimore oriole.

They are about nine inches in height, with narrow sharp bills. The males have black backs and wings, bright orange breasts, black and orange tails. Females are brownish-green above with dark heads and dull orange bellies.

Baltimore orioles migrate to Mexico and South America, and upon their return you can clearly hear the melodious male defending its nesting territory. They forage for insects, primarily caterpillars, and even the hairy ones that other birds often avoid. They feed on sugar water and can be enticed to your yard by offering them berries or sliced oranges at your bird feeder.

They are beautiful nest builders, and weave deep pouches that are suspended from the end of long branches. They are usually quite high, around 30 feet, and found in deciduous trees, like cottonwoods or poplars. Both parents construct the nest as well as feed the nestlings. Even after the young fledge the nest they stay together and feed as a family.

TIP: Look for these fantastic birds in early spring before their migration in late July. In the summer of 2000, female orioles were seen with their offspring looking for food in mixed forest settings near the edge of the park.

SIZE: 8 – 10 inches

HABITAT: Lowland, deciduous and coniferous forests

OCCURRENCE: Winter, common

IDENTIFICATION: Red and gray mottled bird, somewhat tame

PINE GROSBEAK
Pinicola enucleator

Largest of the northern finches with their large black beaks and rosy head, breast and back, the pine grosbeak decorates wintertime pines in Voyageurs National Park for you. Females are of gray and yellow-brassy plumage. About the size of a robin, pine grosbeaks are big, round birds of the north that tolerate the cold winters of Canada and northern Minnesota. If found further south, it seems to be due to lack of food sources. Winter is a good time to spot them, given their red, ornamental coloring against the white snow and green pines. Their big beaks are used to eat the seeds from the mountain ash, cedar, spruce, tamarack, white pine and available fruit including sumac berries and cranberries. Observations of pine grosbeaks suggest it is ultimately the kernel of the seed that is the food they seek, leaving the rest of the fruit or cone in fragments on the ground below them. It is worth taking a trip to the park in the winter to find them perched on a pine. In the summer, they can be found in mixed woodlands with conifers and will be found nesting in a spruce or a fir tree.

Pine grosbeaks are very tame and will stay perched on a branch as you walk by. They will sing in flight, warbling out "tee tee tee."

TIP: Look for them on brushy clearings and forest edges. They prefer coniferous woods. The Echo Bay Trail and the Chain of Lakes Trail are good springtime spots for this grosbeak.

SIZE: 5.5 – 6.5 inches

HABITAT: Deciduous and coniferous forests

OCCURRENCE: Summer, common

IDENTIFICATION: Male is rosy red on the head and rump

PURPLE FINCH
Carpodacus purpureus

This little finch is commonly found in Voyageurs National Park. When looking for it, look for a raspberry-red-colored male and not the purple of its name. The male is mostly colored red, heavily on its head and rump with brown streaks on its back. Both male and female have notched tail. The female has a light brown and white streaked breast, and brown ear patch.

They breed mostly in coniferous and mixed wood forests. Look for a compact cup of twigs, roots, grasses, and moss in a pine tree branch about 15 feet off the ground. Finches feed in trees on seed and buds, on the ground they will eat weed and grass seeds and some caterpillars and beetles.

These birds are gregarious and are known for the male's courtship flight. The female builds the nest and incubates three to five eggs, not leaving the nest until the eggs hatch, this is made easy by the male who feeds her during that time. While these birds are known as forest dwellers, they can be tempted to bird feeders but only if house finches and house sparrows are not present to compete for feeder food.

Its song is a long rich warbling, its call is a musical "chur-lee" and it calls "tic" as it flies. The male will happily sing this in the spring and early summer morning hours.

TIP: Look for small flocks of Purple Finches in second growth woodland and residential areas, such as the Echo Bay Trail, parts of the Blind Ash Bay Trail, and the Black Bay Beaver Pond walk in Black Bay.

SIZE: 5–5.5 inches
HABITAT: Marshes and open water marshes
OCCURRENCE: Winter, common
IDENTIFICATION: Red face and chin, usually in flocks

COMMON REDPOLL
Carduelis flammea

The amazing little common redpoll, and its cousin, the hoary redpoll, can withstand colder temperatures more than any other North American song-bird. They nest on the southern edge of the Arctic tundra. Noted for their tameness, they will often perch very close to you, if you stand quietly while watching them. This, unfortunately, allows predators to attack them more easily.

Common redpolls do not fight over nesting territory, and instead often nest right next to each other.

They are winter visitors to the park, traveling together in large flocks. They vigorously break open dried flower stalks in search of seeds in stands of dead weeds. Like other cold climate finches, large flocks of common redpolls will erupt far south of their normal range in search of food during harsh winters, and can be seen flocking with gold finches and pine siskins.

These are gray-brown birds, smaller than sparrows. They have white breasts with heavy brown streaking, red caps and yellow bills. Males have a pinkish breast patch. The song is a continuous twitter.

TIP: In the winter, walk the edges of frozen wetlands, like Tom Cod Bay and Tilson Bay and Black Bay and look for large flocks of these birds as they pick through dried grass-es. These birds will go anywhere in the park to seek shelter such as forest cover or bury themselves in the snow.

SIZE: 7.5 – 8.5 inches

HABITAT: Coniferous forests

OCCURRENCE: Permanent, common

IDENTIFICATION: Bright yellow eyebrow, brown head diffusing into yellow body

EVENING GROSBEAK
Coccothraustes vespertinus

The translation of the evening grosbeak's Latin generic name, "shatterer of seeds" is a good tip for understanding a key trait to this bird. One of the largest finches and found in Voyageurs Park in the winter, listen for its noisy, loud "clap" or "jeer" in a grove of pine trees.

This eight-inch long, stocky, noisy finch can be found in Voyageurs year-round. Voyageurs National Park is on the southern limit of this bird's breeding habitat. The pines of the boreal forest provide it with its hard-to-find nesting spot. If you walk into a 30 feet tall and higher tree understory, with a soft needle leaf floor, you are in evening grosbeak habitat. The forest-devastating spruce budworm is one of its favorite foods, in addition to tree buds, cedar berries and maple seed. Its large head, conical bill that is gray in winter and green starting in the spring, can pry open the toughest of nuts and seeds. The discarded fruit, along with empty maple seed wings on the ground will alert you to a grosbeak's perch or nest. They drink sap from sapsucker drillings, too.

The male has a yellow body, black crown and tail, and black and white wings. The female has a gray body, yellow napes and sides, and black and white wings.

TIP: Look for evening grosbeaks on the Blind Ash Bay Trail, the Mica Bay Portage or the Little Trout Lake Portage.

SIZE: 5–6.5 inches

HABITAT: Open water, upland shrublands and deciduous forests

OCCURRENCE: Permanent, uncommon

IDENTIFICATION: Black eyestripe, white cheeks, found near human habitation

HOUSE SPARROW
Passer domesticus

Arguably the most familiar bird on the planet, the house sparrow has expanded its range from Eurasia and North Africa to all of the Earth's continents by introduction. Every house sparrow in North America is the descendant of a handful of birds released in New York City's Central Park in 1850.

Quarrelsome and aggressive, they compete with our native songbirds for both food and nest sites, so it is perhaps easy to understand why many people dislike them. They are, however, not to be blamed for being transplanted, and, in fact, are hardy survivors that are compatible with civilization. Although common, they are quite handsome.

House sparrows lay up to three broods of eggs in a season and congregate in noisy, gregarious flocks. They eat almost anything, but enjoy insects and seeds, often monopolizing bird feeders. Nests are made of feathers and debris and are built into just about any cavity, natural or man-made.

House sparrows are small, tan-colored birds, rarely alone and quite approachable. Males have white cheeks, black throats, beaks, and "raccoon masks," gray crowns and rumps, white belly, and otherwise mottled brown. Females and juveniles are a rather indistinct tan, with yellow-brown beaks and tan eye stripes. Their song is a monotonous chirp. They are most often found close to human habitation.

TIP: Look for house sparrows as you first arrive at the park's edge among resorts and entry area camping grounds.

COMPLETE CHECKLIST OF
VOYAGEURS NATIONAL PARK BIRDS
240 Species

Common loon

Red-throated loon

Red-necked grebe

Horned grebe

Western grebe

Pied-billed grebe

White pelican

Double-crested Cormorant

Great blue heron

American bittern

Whistling swan

Canada goose

(Blue) Snow goose

(White) Snow goose

Mallard

Black duck

Gadwall

Pintail

Green-winged teal

Blue-winged teal

American wigeon

Shoveler

Wood duck

Ring-necked duck

Canvasback

Greater scaup

Lesser scaup

Common goldeneye

Bufflehead

Oldsquaw

White-winged scoter

Surf scoter

Ruddy duck

Hooded merganser

Common merganser

Red-breasted merganser

Turkey vulture

Goshawk

Sharp-shinned hawk

Cooper's hawk

Red-tailed hawk

Broad-winged hawk

Rough-legged hawk

Golden eagle

Bald eagle

Northern harrier

Osprey

Gyrfalcon

Peregrine falcon

Merlin

American kestral

Spruce grouse

Ruffed grouse

Sharp-tailed grouse

Sandhill crane

Virginia rail

Sora rail

Yellow rail

American coot

Piping plover

Semipalmated plover

Killdeer

Lesser golden plover

Ruddy turnstone

American woodcock

Common snipe

Upland plover

Spotted sandpiper

Solitary sandpiper

Willet

Greater yellowlegs

Lesser yellowlegs

Pectoral sandpiper

White-rumped sandpiper

Baird's sandpiper

Least sandpiper

Dunlin

Dowitcher

Semipalmated sandpiper

Western sandpiper

Marbled godwit

Hudsonian godwit

Sanderling

Wilson's phalarope

Herring gull

Ring-billed gull

Franklin's gull

Bonaparte's gull

Common tern

Caspian tern

Black tern

Rock dove

Mourning dove

Yellow-billed cuckoo

Black-billed cuckoo

Great horned owl

Snowy owl

Hawk owl

Barred owl

Great grey owl

Long-eared owl

Boreal owl

Saw-whet owl

Whip-poor-will

Common nighthawk

Chimney swift

Rufous hummingbird

Ruby-throated hummingbird

Belted kingfisher

Common flicker

Pileated woodpecker

Red-headed woodpecker

Yellow-bellied sapsucker

Hairy woodpecker

Downy woodpecker

Black-backed three-toed
    Woodpecker

Northern three-toed
    Woodpecker

Eastern kingbird

Great Crested flycatcher

Eastern phoebe

Yellow-bellied flycatcher

Alder flycatcher

Least flycatcher

Eastern wood pewee

Olive-sided flycatcher

Horned lark

Tree swallow

Bank swallow

Rough-winged swallow

Barn swallow

Cliff swallow

Purple martin

Gray jay

Blue jay

Black-billed magpie

Common raven

Common crow

Black-capped chickadee

Boreal chickadee

White-breasted nuthatch

Red-breasted nuthatch

Brown creeper

House wren

Winter wren

Marsh wren

Sedge wren

Mockingbird

Catbird

Brown thrasher

Robin

Wood thrush

Hermit thrush

Swainson's thrush

Gray-cheeked thrush

Veery

Eastern bluebird

Golden-crowned kinglet

Ruby-crowned kinglet

Water pipit

Bohemian waxwing

Cedar waxwing

Northern shrike

Starling

Solitary vireo

Red-eyed vireo

Philadelphia vireo

Warbling vireo

Black-and-white warbler

Golden-winged warbler

Tennessee warbler

Orange-crowned warbler

Nashville warbler

Northern Parula warbler

Yellow warbler

Magnolia warbler

Cape may warbler

Black-throated blue warbler

Yellow-rumped warbler

Black-throated green warbler

Blackburnian warbler

Chestnut-sided warbler

Bay-breasted warbler

Blackpoll warbler

Pine warbler

Ovenbird

Northern waterthrush

Connecticut warbler

Mourning warbler

Common yellowthroat

Wilson's warbler

Canada warbler

American redstart

House sparrow

Bobolink

Eastern meadowlark

Western meadowlark

Yellow-headed blackbird

Red-winged blackbird

Baltimore (northern) oriole

Rusty blackbird

Brewer's blackbird

Common grackle

Brown-headed cowbird

Scarlet tanager

Rose-breasted grosbeak

Indigo bunting

Evening grosbeak

Hoary redpoll

Common redpoll

Pine siskin

American goldfinch

Red crossbill

White-winged crossbill

Rufous-sided towhee

Savannah sparrow

LeConte's sparrow

Vesper sparrow

Dark-eyed (northern or
    slate-colored) junco

Northern (Oregon) junco

Tree sparrow

Chipping sparrow

Clay-colored sparrow

Fox sparrow

Lincoln's sparrow

Swamp sparrow

Song sparrow

Lapland longspur

Snow bunting

Harris' sparrow

White-crowned sparrow

White-throated sparrow

This bibliography includes the works that were used in the research for this guide.

Akins, R. and B. Hilton Jr. *Birds of the Minneapolis-St. Paul Region: A Twin Cities Checklist.* Minneapolis: Minnesota Ornithological Union, 1983.

Benyus, J. M. *Northwoods Wildlife: A Watcher's Guide to Habitats.* Minocqua: NorthWord Press, Inc., 1989.

Bull, J. and J. Farrand Jr. *The Audubon Society Field Guide to North American Birds: Eastern Region.* New York: Alfred A Knopf, Inc.; Toronto: Random House of Canada Ltd., 1977.

Bull, J. and J. Farrand Jr. *The Audubon Society Field Guide to North American Birds: Western Region.* New York: Alfred A Knopf, Inc.; Toronto: Random House of Canada Ltd., 1977.

Bull, J. and J. Farrand Jr. *National Audubon Society Field Guide to North American Birds.* New York: Alfred A. Knopf, Inc., 1994.

Cunningham, R.L. *50 Common Birds of the Southwest.* Tucson: Southwest Parks and Monument Association, 1990.

Dunn J. and K. Garrett. *A Field Guide to Warblers of North America.* Boston: Houghton Mifflin, 1977.

Dunne, P., D. Sibley and C. Sutton. *Hawks In Flight.* Boston: Houghton Mifflin, 1989.

Ehrlich, P.R., D. Dobkin and D. Wheye. *The Birders Handbook.* New York: Simon & Schuster, 1988.

Eriksson, P. and A. Pistorius, Eds. *Treasury of North American Birdlore.* Margaret Morse Nice, "On Watching An Ovenbird's Nest." 1987.

Green, J.C. *Birds and Forests.* St. Paul: Minnesota Department of Natural Resources, 1995.

Green, J.C. and G. J. Neimi. *Birds of the Superior National Forest.* Eastern Region Forest Service, U.S. Department of Agriculture, 1978.

Grigs, J.L. *All the Birds of North America.* New York: HarperCollins, 1997.

Grim, L. *Birds of Voyageurs National Park.* International Falls: Lake States Interpretive Association, 1986.

Heinrich, B. *Mind of the Raven.* New York: HarperCollins, 1999.

Heinrich, B. *Ravens In Winter.* New York: Vintage Books, 1989.

Jaakko Poyry Consulting Inc. *Biodiversity.* "A technical paper for a generic environmental impact statement on timber harvesting and forest management in Minnesota." Report for the Environmental Quality Board, State of Minnesota. 1992.

Janssen, R.B. *Birds in Minnesota.* Minneapolis: University of Minnesota Press, 1987.

Kaufman, K. *Lives of North American Birds.* Boston: Houghton Mifflin, 1996.

Lynch, W. *Northern Birds 1989: Engagement Diary.* Minocqua: NorthWord Press, Inc., 1988.

National Geographic Society. *Field Guide to Birds.* Washington, D.C.: National Geographic Society, 1987.

Oberholtzer, Ernest C., *American Forests and Forest Life.* "The Lakes of Verendrye", on file at the Minnesota Historical Society library, November 1929.

Olson, Sigurd. *The Singing Wilderness.* Minneapolis: University of Minnesota Press, 1997.

Peterson, R.T. A *Field Guide to Western Birds.* Second Edition. Boston: Houghton Mifflin, 1961.

Reader's Digest. *Birds: Their Life, Their Ways, Their World.* Reader's Digest. 1979.

Reiser, M. Hildegard. *Effects of Regulated Lake Levels on the Reproductive Success, Distribution and Abundance of the Aquatic Bird Community in Voyageurs National Park, Minnesota.* Omaha, Nebraska: U.S. Department of the Interior, National Park Service, Research/Resources Management Report MWR-13. Midwest Regional Office, 68102.

Roberts, T.S., M.D. *The Birds of Minnesota.* Minneapolis: University of Minnesota Press, 1936.

Rokach, A. and A. Millman. *A Field Guide to Photographing Birds.* New York: Amphoto Books, 1995.

Stokes, D. *A Guide to Bird Behavior,* Vol. 1. New York: Little, Brown & Co., 1979.

Stokes, D. *A Guide to Bird Behavior,* Vol. 2. New York: Little, Brown & Co., 1983.

Stokes, D. *A Guide to Bird Behavior,* Vol. 3. New York: Little, Brown & Co., 1989.

Stokes D. and L. Stokes. *Stokes Field Guide to Birds of Eastern Region.* Boston: Little, Brown & Co., 1996.

Tekiela, S. *Birds of Minnesota Field Guide.* Cambridge: Adventure Publishing, 1998.

Terres, J.K. *The Audubon Society Encyclopedia of North American Birds.* Avenel, New Jersey: Wing Books, 1995.

Thoreau, Henry. *Thoreau on Birds.* New York: McGraw Hill, 1964.

Turner, A. and C. Rose. *Swallows and Martins: An Identification Guide and Handbook.* Boston: Houghton Mifflin Co., 1991.

U.S. Fish and Wildlife Service. *For the Birds.* U.S. Fish and Wildlife Service, 1997.

Voyageurs National Park, Chippewa National Forest, Nicolet National Forest. *Birds of the Lake States.* International Falls: Lake States Interpretive Association.

Welden Owen Production. *Encyclopedia of Birds.* New York: Smithmark, 1991.

Actitis macularia: 38
Agelaius phoeniceus: 106
American goldeneye: 28
American kestrel: 34
American redstart: 89
American robin: 77
American tree sparrow: 94
American white pelican: 19
American woodcock: 40
Ammodramus leconteii: 98
Anas platyrhynchos: 24
Archilochus colubris: 46
Ardea herodias: 21
Ash River beaver pond trail: 54, 106
Ash River resort: 66
Ash River road: 44, 108
Ash River trail: 85, 89, 91, 96
Audubon's warbler: 85
Aythya affinis: 27
Aythya collaris: 25
Aythya marila: 26
Bald eagle: 22, 32, 41
Baltimore oriole: 109
Barn swallow: 67
Barred owl: 44
Belted kingfisher: 47
Birch warblers: 81
Black Bay: 16, 17, 18, 21, 23, 24, 25, 27, 28, 112
Black Bay Beaver Pond walk: 54, 111
Black-and-white creeper: 88
Black-and-white warbler: 88
Black-backed, three-toed woodpecker: 51
Black-capped chickadee: 68
Black-throated green warbler: 86
Blackpoll warbler: 87
Blind Ash Bay trail: 49, 50, 84, 92, 111, 113
Blue jay: 47, 48, 62, 107
Bog walk at Orr: 85, 91
Bombycilla cedrorum: 80
Branta canadensis: 23
Brewer's sparrow: 96
Broad-winged hawk: 33
Brown thrasher: 79
Brown-headed cowbird: 82, 108
Bucephala clangula: 28
Bullet-hawk: 35
Bullock's oriole: 109

Buteo platypterus: 33
Calaveras warblers: 81
Canada goose: 23
Cardinals: 79
Carduelis flammea: 112
Carpodacus purpureus: 111
Cathartes aura: 22
Catharus fuscescens: 74
Catharus guttatus: 76
Catharus ustulatus: 75
Cedar waxwing: 80
Ceryle alcyon: 47
Chain of Lakes trail: 27, 47, 54, 60, 61, 81, 84, 90, 103, 110
Charadrius vociferus: 37
Chestnut-sided warbler: 83
Chickadee: 81, 84, 85, 87, 89, 91, 92
Chipping sparrow: 95, 96
Chordeiles minor: 45
Cistothorus platensis: 71
Clay-colored Sparrow: 96
Cliff swallow: 66
Coccothraustes vespertinus: 113
Colaptes auratus: 52
Common crow: 58
Common flicker: 77, 79, 107
Common grackle: 35, 52, 77, 107
Common loon: 15
Common Merganser: 29, 30
Common nighthawk: 45
Common or American crow: 58, 63
Common or northern flicker: 52
Common Raven: 63, 64
Common redpoll: 112
Common snipe: 39
Common tern: 43
Connecticut warbler: 91
Contopus virens: 54
Cormorants: 19
Corvus brachyrhynchos: 63
Corvus corax: 64
Cranberry Bay: 16, 17, 18, 21, 23, 25, 29, 31
Crane Lake: 67
Cruiser Lake: 61, 80
Cruiser Lake trail: 47, 54, 60, 81, 89, 106
Cyanocitta cristata: 62
Dark-eyed (slate-colored or northern) junco: 104
Dendroica coronata: 85

Dendroica magnolia: 84
Dendroica pensylvanica: 83
Dendroica petechia: 82
Dendroica striata: 87
Dendroica virens: 86
Double-crested cormorant: 19, 20
Downy woodpecker: 49, 50
Drycopus pileatus: 53
Duck Bay: 16, 17, 18, 21, 23, 24, 25, 29
Dumetella carolinensis: 78
Eared grebes: 17
Eastern kingbird: 58
Eastern phoebe: 56
Eastern wood-pewee: 54
Echo Bay: 31
Echo Bay trail: 40, 46, 52, 53, 54, 57,
    59, 71, 73, 78, 84, 87, 88, 92, 96, 98,
    105, 108, 110, 111
Empidonax minimus: 55
Evening grosbeak: 113
Falcipennis canadensis: 36
Falco columbarius: 35
Falco sparverius: 34
Finches: 35, 104, 105, 110, 112, 113
Fish hawk: 31
Fool's hen: 36
Fox sparrow: 99
Gallinago gallinago: 39
Gavia immer: 15
Gold finches: 112
Gold Portage: 37, 47
Golden-crowned kinglet: 72
Grassy Bay: 16, 17, 18, 21, 23, 24, 25,
    28, 29, 31
Grassy Islands: 28
Gray catbird: 78
Gray jay: 61
Great blue heron: 21
Great grey owl: 44
Great horned owl: 43
Great-crested flycatcher: 57
Greater scaup: 26, 27
Hairy woodpecker: 49, 50, 52
Haliaeetus leucocephalus: 32
Hawks: 58
Hermit thrush: 74, 75, 76, 99
Herring gull: 41, 42
Hirundo rustica: 67
Hoary redpoll: 112
Hooded merganser: 29

Horned grebe: 17
House finches: 111
House sparrow: 80, 107, 111, 114
House wren: 70
Icterus galbula: 109
Junco hyemalis: 104
Kabetogama Lake Road: 44
Kabetogama Peninsula: 59, 74, 75
Kestrel: 35
Kestrels: 107
Kettle Falls: 65
Killdeer: 37
Larus argentatus: 42
Larus delawarensis: 41
Le Conte's sparrow: 98
Least flycatcher: 55
Lesser scaup: 26, 27
Little blue bill: 27
Little fish duck: 29
Little Trout Lake Portage: 113
Lophodytes cucullatus: 29
Lost Bay: 31
MacGillivray's warbler: 92
Magnolia warbler: 84
Mallard: 24
Mariposas: 89
Melospiza georgiana: 101
Melospiza melodia: 100
Mergus merganser: 30
Merlin: 35
Mica Bay: 36
Mica Bay Portage: 113
Mica Bay trail: 65, 80
Mniotilta varia: 88
Mockingbird: 78, 79
Molothrus ater: 108
Mourning Warbler: 92
Myiarchus crinitus: 57
Myrtle warbler: 85
Nashville swamp warblers: 81
Nashville warbler: 81
Northern flicker: 50
Northern oriole: 109
Nuthatch: 73, 88
Oberholtzer trail: 39, 44, 52, 71, 82, 84,
    87, 88, 98, 101, 103
Oporornis agilis: 91
Oporornis philadelphia: 92
Osprey: 31, 32
Ovenbird: 90

Pandion haliaetus: 31
Passer domesticus: 114
Passerculus sandwichensis: 97
Passerella iliaca: 99
Pelicanus erythrorhynchos: 19
Peninsula trails: 82, 87, 101
Perisoreus canadensis: 61
Petrpchelidon pyrrhonota: 66
Phalacrocorax auritus: 20
Pheucticus ludovicianus: 105
Picoides arcticus: 51
Picoides pubescens: 49
Picoides tridactylus: 51
Picoides villosus: 50
Pied creeper: 88
Pied-billed grebe: 16
Pigeons: 35
Pileated woodpecker: 53
Pine grosbeak: 110
Pine siskins: 112
Pinicola enucleator: 110
Piranga olivacea: 93
Podiceps auritus: 17
Podiceps grisegena: 18
Podilymbus podiceps: 16
Poecile atricapillus: 68
Purple finch: 111
Quiscalus quiscula: 107
Rainy Lake Visitor Center: 65, 66, 106
Raven: 33
Ravens: 58
Red-breasted nuthatch: 69
Red-eyed vireo: 59, 60, 90
Red-necked grebe: 18
Red-winged blackbird: 106
Regulus calendula: 73
Regulus satrapa: 72
Ring-billed duck: 25
Ring-billed gull: 41
Ring-necked duck: 25
Robin: 61, 78, 79, 107, 108, 110
Rose-breasted grosbeak: 105
Ruby-crowned kinglet: 73
Ruby-throated hummingbird: 46
Savannah sparrow: 97, 98
Sayornis phoebe: 56
Scarlet tanager: 93
Scolopax minor: 40
Sedge wren: 71
Seiurus aurocapillus: 90

Setophaga ruticilla: 89
Sheep Islands: 43
Sitta canadensis: 69
Song sparrow: 97, 100, 101
Sparrow: 35, 104, 112
Sphyrapicus varius: 48
Spizella arborea: 94
Spizella pallida: 96
Spizella passerina: 95
Spotted sandpiper: 37, 38
Spruce grouse: 36
Sterna hirundo: 43
Strix varia: 44
Sullivan Bay: 31, 94
Swainson's thrush: 75, 76
Swamp sparrow: 101
Tachycineta bicolor: 65
Teeter snipe: 38
Three-toed woodpecker: 51
Tilson Bay: 112
Tilson Creek trail: 59
Tom Cod: 17
Tom Cod Bay: 21, 94, 112
Toxostoma rufum: 79
Tree sparrow: 94
Tree swallow: 65
Trogolodytes aedon: 70
Turdus migratorious: 77
Turkey vulture: 22
Tyrannus tyrannus: 58
Veery: 74, 75, 76
Vermilion Gorge: 105
Vermilion Gorge trail: 44, 49, 57, 59, 88
Vermivora ruficapilla: 81
Vireo gilvus: 59
Vireo olivaceus: 60
Vultures: 58
Warbler: 59, 68, 70, 73
Warbling vireo: 59
Whip-poor-will: 45
White-crowned sparrow: 103
White-throated sparrow: 102, 103
Yellow warbler: 82
Yellow-bellied sapsucker: 48
Yellow-rumped warbler: 85
Zonotrichia albicollis: 102
Zonotrichia leucophrys: 103

The Voyageurs Region National Park Association is grateful to the following artists, photographers and institutions for their permission to reproduce the artwork and photographs on the indicated pages. Thank you also to Color Unlimited, Minneapolis, Minnesota for assisting us with Wally Dayton and Nils Rahn's photos.

Ed Bock: 32

Cornell Lab of Ornithology: Betty Darling Cottrille, 59, 91; Chris Crowley, 20; Allen Cruickshank, 63; John Dunning, 78; Bill Dyer, 74, 75, 81; E. Greene, 17; Lang Elliot, 29, 43; John Heidecker, 35, 87; Mike Hopiak, 25, 54, 58, 60, 72, 95, 101; Uve Hublitz, 26, 55; Isidor Jenklin, 42, 57, 61, 66, 76, 84, 88; Lee Kuhn, cover, 22; William Paff, 83; O.S. Pettingill, 65; Johann Schumacher, 85, 100; M&B Schwarzchild, 96; Ted Willcox, 52; J.R. Woodward, 80

Wally Dayton: v, xiii, xvii, 21, 47

Kate Eifler: 13 (lower drawing)

Susan Hilber: xi

Jennifer R. S. Hunt: 19

Bill Marchel: 15, 16, 18, 23, 27, 28, 30, 31, 34, 37, 46, 50, 62, 69, 70, 73, 77, 79, 82, 94, 97, 98, 99, 102, 103, 104, 106, 108, 109, 111, 112, 113, 114

Warren Nelson: 24, 33, 36, 38, 39, 40, 41, 44, 45, 48, 49, 51, 53, 56, 64, 67, 68, 71, 86, 89, 90, 92, 93, 105, 107, 110

John Pastor: 1-5

Nils Rahn: postcard

Matt Schmidt: inside covers, 13 (upper drawing)

Tony Vavricka: xv

Voyageurs National Park: 10-11

Voyageurs Region National Park Association archives by Larry Edwards, vi

Nancy Albrecht

Nancy Albrecht is an ecologist who enjoys looking at plants and listening to birds, preferably from the stern of her canoe. Over her career, she has worked in the area of natural resource management for a variety of public agencies, including Voyageurs National Park, and has volunteered for a variety of conservation-oriented nonprofit organizations. She is currently an employee of the Minnesota Department of Natural Resources. She holds an M.S. in Botany from the University of Minnesota and a B.S. in Botany and Zoology from the University of Wisconsin-Madison.

Kate Eifler

Kate Eifler is a sign language interpreter at the University of Minnesota, and became interested in birding 10 years ago while working in Costa Rica. She worked on an eight month research project studying long-tailed manakins for a doctoral student. The rain forest was a playground for birders where she became an active and enthusiastic participant.

Leland H. Grim

Lee Grim, biology professor and ornithology instructor at the Rainy River Community College in International Falls from 1967-2000, is a seasonal resources biologist at Voyageurs National Park, working there since 1973.

Jennifer Scott Hunt

Jennifer Hunt has been the Executive Director of the Voyageurs Region National Park Association for 14 years and spends her time working on issues related to Voyageurs National Park. It is through her work that she has learned the value and the wonder of the parks' birds. She lives in Minneapolis with her daughters, Kate and Sarah.

John Pastor

John Pastor is professor of biology at the University of Minnesota in Duluth. He teaches animal behavior, ecosystems ecology, mathematical ecology, and biological illustration. He draws birds and is a fair-to-middling bird watcher.

Matt Schmidt

Matt Schmidt has dedicated his waking hours to the preservation of nature. Through illustration and writing, he hopes to cultivate respect for the wilderness and its denizens. He resides in Minneapolis, Minnesota with his wife Stephanie.

VOYAGEURS REGION NATIONAL PARK ASSOCIATION

The mission of the Voyageurs Region National Park Association is to preserve, encourage and promote the natural, recreational and historical resources of Voyageurs National Park in accordance with the park's enabling legislation; and in addition, to be a friend to other National Park Service-managed lands in the region.

For information on the association, contact:

Voyageurs Region National Park Association
514 North Third Street, Ste. 104
Minneapolis, Minnesota 55401-1292
Phone number: 612-333-5424
Email: vrnpa@voyageurs.org
Web site: www.voyageurs.org